QUICK & EASY
PASTA

QUICK & EASY
PASTA

FABULOUS FAST
FOOD ITALIAN STYLE

Consultant Editor: Linda Fraser

Sebastian Kelly

First published in 1999 by Sebastian Kelly
2 Rectory Road, Oxford OX4 1BW

© Anness Publishing Limited 1999

Produced by Anness Publishing Limited
Hermes House, 88–89 Blackfriars Road, London SE1 8HA

ISBN 1 84081 156 0

A CIP catalogue record for this book is available from the British Library.

Publisher: Joanna Lorenz
Senior Cookery Editor: Linda Fraser
Cookery Editors: Rosemary Wilkinson, Linda Doeser
Copy Editor: Val Barrett
Designers: Bill Mason, Siân Keogh
Front cover: Lisa Tai, Designer; Thomas Odulate Photographer;
Helen Trent, Stylist; Lucy McKelvie, Home Economist

Recipes: Catherine Atkinson, Carla Capalbo, Maxine Clark, Roz Denny, Christine France, Sarah Gates,
Shirley Gill, Norma MacMillan, Sue Maggs, Elizabeth Martin, Annie Nichols, Jenny Stacy, Liz Trigg,
Laura Washburn, Steven Wheeler
Photographs: Karl Adamson, Edward Allwright, David Armstrong, Steve Baxter, Jo Brewer,
James Duncan, Michelle Garrett, Amanda Heywood, Patrick McLeavey, Michael Michaels
Stylists: Madeleine Brehaut, Jo Brewer, Carla Capalbo, Michelle Garrett, Hilary Guy, Amanda Heywood,
Patrick McLeavey, Blake Minton, Kirsty Rawlings, Elizabeth Wolf-Cohen
Food for Photography: Wendy Lee, Lucy McElvie, Jane Stevenson, Elizabeth Wolf-Cohen
Illustrator: Anna Koska

Previously published as part of a larger compendium, *Best-Ever Pasta*

Printed and bound in Hong Kong/China

1 3 5 7 9 10 8 6 4 2

NOTES
For all recipes, quantities are given in both metric and imperial measures and, where appropriate,
measures are given in standard cups and spoons. Follow one set, but not a mixture, because
they are not interchangeable.
Standard spoon and cup measurements are level: 1 tsp = 5ml; 1 tbsp = 15ml; 1 cup = 250ml/8fl oz
Australian standard tablespoons are 20ml. Australian readers should use 3 tsp in place of 1 tbsp for
measuring small quantities of gelatine, cornflour, salt, etc.
Medium eggs should be used unless otherwise stated.

CONTENTS

Introduction

Popular with all ages, pasta is the perfect food for cooks in a hurry.
It can be cooked in minutes and served with easy and delicious
sauces made – just as fast – from either store-cupboard or fresh
ingredients. All the recipes in this book can be prepared in
20 minutes or less – and they will probably be eaten just as quickly.

There are dishes for all occasions and courses. Chicken with
Buckwheat Noodle Soup or Spaghetti with Feta Cheese from Soups
& Starters will certainly stimulate the appetite and get the gastric
juices flowing. Fish & Meat Dishes offers a tasty collection of recipes
ideal for midweek family suppers when time is short – from Linguine
with Clam and Tomato Sauce to Fettuccine with Ham and Cream.
For Vegetarian Dishes, pasta is hard to beat, and both vegetarians and
meat-eaters will enjoy such speedy specialities as Pasta Rapido with
Parsley Pesto, Pasta Bows with Fennel and Walnut, and Mushroom
and Chilli Carbonara. Spend time with your guests and not in the
kitchen by choosing recipes from Special Occasion Dishes, such as
Tagliatelle with Saffron Mussels, and Spinach and Ricotta Conchiglie.
Finally, Salads, whether served as an accompaniment or a main
course, offer something special for every season, from Warm Pasta
Salad with Ham and Egg to Pasta, Melon and Prawn Salad.

A comprehensive introduction to a wide range of ingredients, as well
as hints and tips throughout the book, virtually guarantee success,
ensuring that all the recipes are as easy as they are quick.

Types of Pasta

When buying dried pasta, choose good-quality, well-known brands. Of the fresh pasta sold in sealed packs in supermarkets, the filled or stuffed varieties are the ones most worth buying; noodles and ribbon pasta are better bought dried, as these tend to have more bite when cooked. However, if you are lucky enough to live near an Italian delicatessen where pasta is made on the premises, it will usually be of very good quality.

You will see from this book that the recipes are almost limitless in their variety, as are the pasta shapes themselves. There are no hard-and-fast rules regarding which shape of pasta to use with which dish; it is really a matter of personal preference. However, there are a few guidelines to help: long thin pasta suits seafood sauces, while thicker varieties are good with creamy sauces, and thick tubular pasta, such as rigatoni and penne, is best with rustic sauces full of chunky pieces that can be caught in the pasta itself.

Various forms of noodle or pasta are found in China and Japan, but also throughout Malaysia, Hong Kong, and the rest of East Asia, including parts of India and Tibet. Pasta may well have been invented in China.

This pasta, usually in the form of noodles and often enhanced with a sprinkling of vegetables or fish, adds variety to the sometimes monotonous staple diet of rice and beans eaten by the poorer sections of the population. Some types of pasta are used to give bulk to soups; others are eaten as a filling dish to stave off hunger during the day. They are made from the staple crops of each

region – whether rice flour, soya bean flour, or potato flour – and are cooked in different ways: some are soaked and then fried, some are boiled and fried, and some are rolled out and stuffed like ravioli, but most are simply boiled. Some turn transparent when cooked.

Egg noodles are usually made with wheat flour and can be treated in the same way as Western pasta. Buckwheat and fresh whole-wheat noodles are similarly cooked. Fresh white noodles do not contain egg, but are cooked in the same way as egg noodles. Some dried egg noodles come in discs or blocks and are "cooked" by immersion in boiling water, in which they are then left to soak for a few minutes. As with Western pasta, Eastern noodles can be flavoured with other ingredients, such as prawns, carrot or spinach. Wonton wrappers, like thin squares of rolled-out pasta, are used for stuffing and making filled shapes. Although Eastern pasta is available in a variety of long noodle types, it does not seem to be made into the shapes that we are used to seeing in the West: you will often find it wound into balls and beautifully packaged.

Right: It is estimated that there are more than 200 different pasta shapes with at least 600 names. Names vary just from region to region in Italy, and new shapes are being designed all the time.

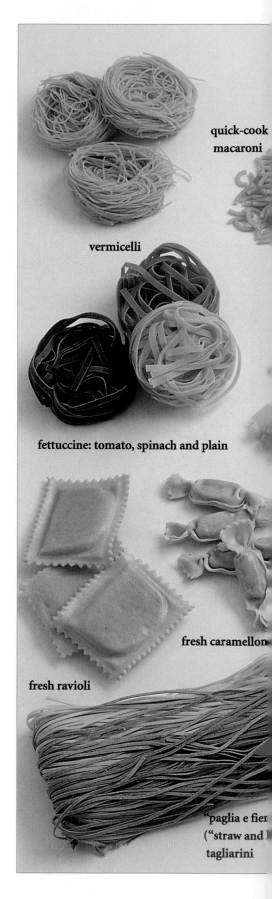

quick-cook macaroni

vermicelli

fettuccine: tomato, spinach and plain

fresh caramellon

fresh ravioli

"paglia e fien ("straw and l tagliarini

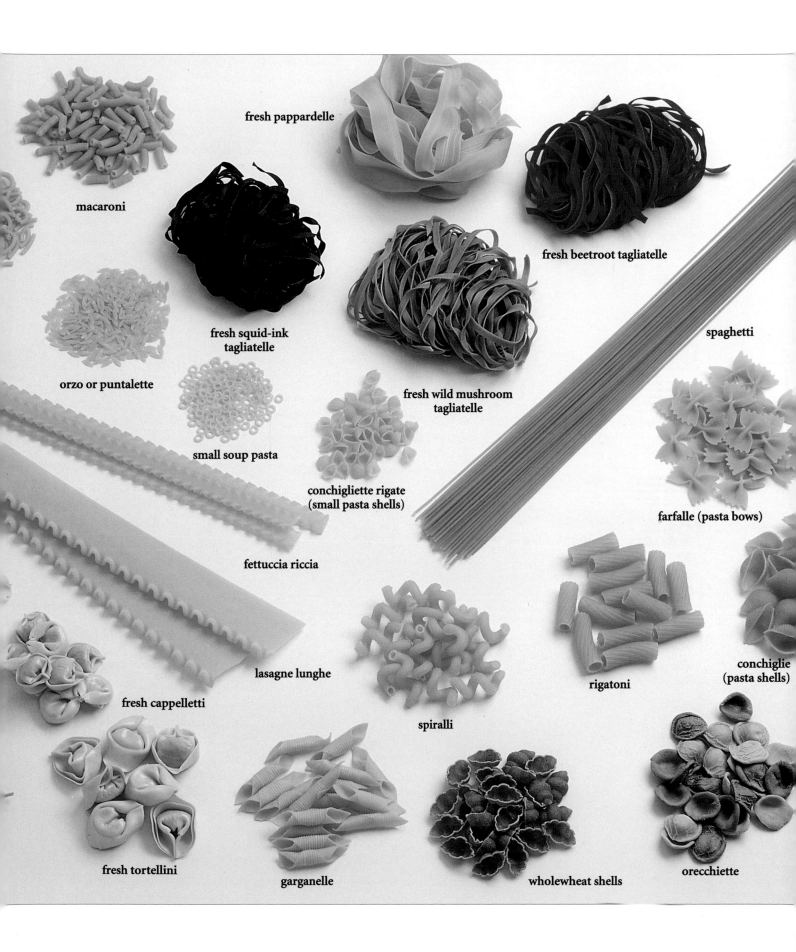

macaroni

fresh pappardelle

fresh beetroot tagliatelle

fresh squid-ink
tagliatelle

spaghetti

orzo or puntalette

fresh wild mushroom
tagliatelle

small soup pasta

conchigliette rigate
(small pasta shells)

farfalle (pasta bows)

fettuccia riccia

rigatoni

conchiglie
(pasta shells)

lasagne lunghe

fresh cappelletti

spiralli

fresh tortellini

garganelle

wholewheat shells

orecchiette

Herbs and Spices

Fresh chillies

Garlic

Basil

Nutmeg

Both fresh and dried herbs can be used successfully to enhance the flavour of most pasta sauces.

Ideally, use fresh herbs immediately after cutting, but most will store well in a jar of water covered with a sealed plastic bag and placed in the fridge.

Dried herbs are very useful, provided they are not too old. Freeze-dried are the best, as they retain both colour and flavour. Use half the quantity of dried herbs as you would fresh, for the flavour is more concentrated.

Basil
Fresh basil is *the* herb for pasta dishes, and dried basil is a poor substitute. The flavour is a pungent mixture of cinnamon and anise, and is wonderful with tomatoes and in delicate ricotta cheese fillings. It is lost, however, in hearty meat sauces. Basil is the main ingredient of pesto. If fresh basil is unavailable, use a spoonful of ready-made pesto instead of dried basil for a better flavour.

Bay leaves
Bay leaves are used to enhance the flavour of meat sauces and to give a delicate flavour to béchamel or white sauces.

Chillies (fresh and dried)
Use smaller quantities of dried chillies than fresh – they add heat to sauces. Wear protective gloves when preparing or work under running water. Do not rub your eyes, as the juice of both dried and fresh chillies can be painful.

Dill
A herb with a slightly aniseed flavour which marries well with fish. It is especially good with fresh or smoked salmon.

Garlic
Garlic is a marvellous flavour enhancer. It is good in dishes where a strong onion taste is required – meat sauces, anything with tomato and with pulses.

Nutmeg
Nutmeg gives a rich, musky flavour to white sauces and is excellent with cheese.

Oregano and marjoram
Together with basil and sage, these are the most popular herbs used in Italy. They have an affinity with tomatoes and eggs, and make a pretty garnish when in flower.

Parsley (curly and flat-leaf)
Parsley is a very versatile herb and both types of parsley impart a fresh "green" flavour to almost any dish. The common curly variety is good for chopping and the flat-leaf one is lovely used as a garnish.

Rocket
Rocket, with its slightly peppery taste, can be used as both a herb and as a salad ingredient. Simply stir a handful of rocket into a pasta dish before just serving.

Saffron
This is one of the world's most expensive spices. This delicate spice will impart a wonderful aroma and colour to any dish.

Sage
A classic Italian herb available in many varieties. It has a lovely earthy flavour and is good with meat and some cheeses.

Sauces and Flavourings

There is an infinite variety of ready-made sauces, pastes, and flavourings available, which you can add to your own sauce to give it a richer or deeper flavour.

Anchovies (salted)
Whole anchovies preserved in salt are sometimes available. They need to be rinsed and the backbone removed before use. They have a fresher flavour than canned anchovy fillets in oil. Used in moderation, anchovies add a fishy depth to sauces and soups.

Capers
These are little green flower buds picked before they open and preserved in vinegar or salt. They add a sharp piquancy to rich sauces and are particularly good with tomatoes and cheese.

Carbonara sauce
Although your own version made from the recipe in this book will be much better, ready-made carbonara sauce is a useful standby for a quick weekday meal. You can add mushrooms or more bacon, ham or pancetta, if wished.

Chopped garlic
A great time-saver, eliminating the need for peeling and chopping. Use it straight from the jar.

Mushroom paste
Add a generous spoonful to freshly cooked pasta, together with a little cream, for a quick sauce.

Olive paste
Delicious stirred into hot pasta with chopped fresh tomatoes or added by the spoonful to enrich a tomato or meat sauce.

Passata
A useful store-cupboard item, this is pulped tomato that has been strained to remove the seeds. It makes a good base for a smooth tomato sauce, although canned plum tomatoes can also be used.

Pesto
Brands vary, but it is a very useful store-cupboard standby to stir into hot pasta and soups.

Pesto (fresh)
Some supermarkets produce their own "fresh" pesto, available in tubs in the chill cabinet. This is infinitely superior to the bottled variety, although your own freshly made pesto will be even better.

Tomato pasta sauce
A good standby or base for a quick meal. Vary by adding chopped anchovies and olives, or pour over freshly cooked stuffed pasta.

Tomato purée
This is an essential if you are making a sauce from insipid fresh tomatoes! It will intensify any tomato-based sauce and will also help thicken meat sauces.

Tomatoes (canned chopped)
Usually made from Italian plum tomatoes which have a fuller flavour than most, these are the heart of a good tomato sauce if you cannot find really ripe, red, tasty fresh tomatoes.

Tomatoes (sun-dried in oil)
These tomatoes are preserved in oil. To use, drain and chop and add to tomato-based recipes to give a deeper, almost roasted tomato flavour to the dish.

Salted anchovies

Chopped garlic

Olive paste

Sun-dried tomatoes in oil

Basic Sauce Ingredients

Onion

Pine nuts

Gorgonzola

Peppers

Artichokes (globe)
Freshly cooked or canned artichoke hearts are excellent tossed with pasta, other vegetable ingredients and a dressing for a quick pasta salad.

Clams
These tiny shellfish are used to make sauces and soups. Fresh cockles are a good substitute, as are canned clams in brine.

Dolcelatte
An Italian, blue-veined, creamy cheese used in sauces and fillings.

Feta
Feta is a firm and crumbly cheese with a salty taste.

Gorgonzola
An Italian, blue-veined, semi-soft cheese with a piquant flavour, used in sauces and stuffings.

Italian sausages
These meaty, highly-seasoned fresh sausages are used to make quick sauces and stuffings.

Mussels
Mussels are best fresh, but frozen cooked ones can be substituted.

Olives
Used in sauces to add richness, black olives have the most flavour.

Onions
Spanish onions add sweetness, and red or purple types add a mild flavour and attractive colour.

Pancetta
Italian bacon, sold smoked or unsmoked, sliced or in one piece, is used to add flavour to sauces.

Parmesan
Good for grating, this hard cheese is made from low-fat, unpasteurized cow's milk.

Peppers
Red, yellow and green peppers make a delicious addition to a sauce and are good with cold pasta salad.

Pine nuts
These small creamy-coloured nuts are essential in pesto.

Pistachios
These pale green nuts are also used in sweet dishes.

Prawns
Large Mediterranean prawns have more flavour than smaller varieties.

Ricotta
An Italian whey cheese which is soft and creamy.

Smoked salmon
Cold smoked salmon is delicious in sauces and fillings. Slice it thinly before adding to a dish.

Spinach
This leafy vegetable combines especially well with ricotta.

Tomatoes
Choose only really ripe tomatoes – plum if possible. Miniature or cherry tomatoes make a good addition to sauces.

Walnuts
Walnut pesto is a delicious variation, and walnuts provide a crunchy texture in a variety of savoury dishes.

Cooking Pasta

Both fresh and dried pasta are cooked in the same way. The golden rules for success are: use plenty of water and keep checking the pasta to be sure it does not overcook. It should be tender, but still firm to the bite. In Italian, this is known as *al dente*.

Fresh pasta cooks much faster than dried. Some very thin types are ready virtually the moment the water returns to the boil. The following are guidelines for timing pasta, but keep checking. Remember, time the cooking from the moment the water returns to the boil.

Filled pasta
Fresh: 8–10 minutes
Dried: 15–20 minutes

Unfilled pasta
Fresh: 2–3 minutes
Dried: 8–12 minutes

1 Bring a very large saucepan of salted water to the boil. Use at least 4 litres/7 pints/16 cups of water and 10ml/2 tsp salt for every 450g/1lb of pasta. Add 15ml/ 1 tbsp olive oil to prevent the shapes or strands from sticking together. Drop in the pasta all at once and stir well to separate the shapes or strands.

2 If you are cooking spaghetti or other long pasta strands, put the ends in the water and allow them to soften slightly, and then gently push in the remaining lengths as soon as you can.

3 Bring the water back to the boil, reduce the heat slightly, and boil until the pasta is tender, but still firm to the bite. To test, lift a piece of pasta out of the pan with a slotted spoon or long-handled fork and cut it in half. There should be no sign of opaque, uncooked pasta in the centre. Alternatively, cool the pasta slightly and then bite it to check if it is *al dente*.

4 Drain the pasta well in a colander, shaking it vigorously to remove all excess water. Serve at once as the pasta will continue to cook in its own heat.

Above: The equipment needed for preparing a vast range of pasta dishes can be found in most kitchens.

COOK'S TIP

If you are going to cook the pasta further, by baking it in a lasagne, for example, undercook it slightly at this first stage. Pasta for salad should also be slightly undercooked, so that it will not become soggy when it is mixed with the dressing.

SOUPS & STARTERS

Pasta, Parmesan and Cauliflower Soup

A silky smooth, mildly cheesy soup which isn't overpowered by the cauliflower. It makes an elegant dinner-party soup served with crisp Melba toast.

INGREDIENTS

Serves 6

1 large cauliflower
1.2 litres/2 pints/5 cups chicken or
    vegetable stock
175g/6oz farfalle
150ml/¼ pint/⅔ cup single cream or milk
freshly grated nutmeg
pinch of cayenne pepper
60ml/4 tbsp freshly grated
    Parmesan cheese
salt and ground black pepper

For the Melba toast
3–4 slices day-old white bread
freshly grated Parmesan cheese,
    for sprinkling
1.5ml/¼ tsp paprika

3 Add the pasta to the stock and simmer for 10 minutes until tender. Drain, reserve the pasta, and pour the liquid over the cauliflower. Add the cream or milk, nutmeg and cayenne to the cauliflower. Blend until smooth, then press through a sieve. Stir in the cooked pasta. Reheat the soup and stir in the Parmesan. Taste and adjust the seasoning if necessary.

4 Meanwhile make the Melba toast. Preheat the oven to 180°C/350°F/Gas 4. Toast the bread lightly on both sides. Quickly cut off the crusts and split each slice in half horizontally. Scrape off any doughy bits and sprinkle with Parmesan and paprika. Place on a baking sheet and bake in the oven for about 10–15 minutes or until uniformly golden. Serve with the soup.

1 Cut the leaves and central stalk away from the cauliflower and discard. Divide the cauliflower into similar-size florets.

2 Bring the stock to the boil and add the cauliflower. Simmer for about 10 minutes or until very soft. Remove the cauliflower with a slotted spoon and place in a blender or food processor.

Fresh Pea and Ham Soup with Pasta

Frozen peas provide flavour, freshness and colour in this delicious winter soup, which is filling enough to make a light main course or can be served as a starter.

INGREDIENTS

Serves 4

115g/4oz small pasta shapes

30ml/2 tbsp vegetable oil

1 small bunch spring onions, chopped

350g/12oz/3 cups frozen peas

1.2 litres/2 pints/5 cups chicken stock

225g/8oz raw unsmoked ham or gammon

60ml/4 tbsp double cream

salt and ground black pepper

warm crusty bread, to serve

1 Cook the small pasta shapes in plenty of boiling salted water according to the packet instructions. Drain through a colander, place in the pan again, cover with cold water and set aside until required.

2 Heat the vegetable oil in a large heavy saucepan and cook the spring onions gently until soft but not browned. Add the frozen peas and chicken stock, then simmer gently over a low heat for about 10 minutes.

3 Process the soup in a blender or food processor then return to the saucepan. Cut the ham or gammon into short fingers and add, with the pasta, to the saucepan. Simmer for 2–3 minutes and season to taste. Stir in the double cream and serve immediately with the warm crusty bread.

Chicken and Buckwheat Noodle Soup

Buckwheat or soba noodles are widely enjoyed in Japan. The simplest way of serving them is in a hot seasoned broth. Almost any topping can be added and the variations are endless.

INGREDIENTS

Serves 4

225g/8oz skinless, boneless
  chicken breasts
120ml/4fl oz/½ cup soy sauce
15ml/1 tbsp sake
1 litre/1¾ pints/4 cups chicken stock
2 pieces young leek, cut into 2.5cm/
  1in pieces
175g/6oz spinach leaves
300g/11oz buckwheat or soba noodles
sesame seeds, toasted, to garnish

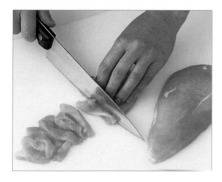

1 Slice the chicken diagonally into bite-size pieces. Combine the soy sauce and sake in a saucepan and bring to a simmer. Add the chicken and cook gently for about 3 minutes, until tender. Keep hot.

2 Bring the stock to the boil in a saucepan. Add the leek and simmer for 3 minutes, then add the spinach. Remove from the heat and keep warm.

3 Cook the buckwheat noodles in a large saucepan of boiling water until just tender, following the packet instructions.

4 Drain the noodles and divide among individual serving bowls. Ladle the hot soup into the bowls, then add a portion of chicken to each. Serve at once, sprinkled with sesame seeds.

COOK'S TIP

Home-made chicken stock makes the world of difference to noodle soup. Put about 1.5kg/3–3½lb meaty chicken bones into a large saucepan, add 3 litres/5 pints/12½ cups water and bring to the boil, skimming off any foam. Add 2 slices fresh root ginger, 2 garlic cloves, 2 celery sticks, 4 spring onions, some coriander stalks and about 10 peppercorns, crushed. Reduce the heat and simmer for 2–2½ hours. Remove from the heat and leave to cool, uncovered and undisturbed, then strain.

Red Pasta Soup

This beautiful, vivid ruby-red soup will look stunning at any dinner-party table.

INGREDIENTS

INGREDIENTS

Serves 4–6

15ml/1 tbsp olive oil

350g/12oz red onions, sliced

2 garlic cloves, crushed

275g/10oz cooked beetroot, cut into sticks

1.2 litres/2 pints/5 cups vegetable stock
    or water

50g/2oz cooked soup pasta

30ml/2 tbsp raspberry vinegar

salt and ground black pepper

low-fat yogurt or fromage blanc,
    to garnish

snipped chives, to garnish

3 Add the beetroot, stock or water, cooked soup pasta and vinegar, and heat through. Season to taste with salt and pepper.

4 Ladle into warmed soup bowls. Top each one with a spoonful of low-fat yogurt or fromage blanc and sprinkle with chives.

1 Heat the olive oil in a flame-proof casserole and add the onions and garlic.

2 Cook gently for 20 minutes or until the onions and garlic are soft and tender.

Chicken Vermicelli Soup with Egg Shreds

This soup is very quick and easy – you can add all sorts of extra ingredients to vary the taste, using up leftovers such as spring onions, mushrooms, a few prawns or chopped salami.

INGREDIENTS

Serves 4–6

3 eggs

30ml/2 tbsp chopped fresh coriander or parsley

1.5 litres/2½ pints/6¼ cups good chicken stock or canned consommé

115g/4oz dried vermicelli or angel hair pasta

115g/4oz cooked chicken breast, sliced

salt and ground black pepper

1 First make the egg shreds. Whisk the eggs together in a small bowl and stir in the coriander or parsley.

2 Heat a small non-stick frying pan and pour in 30–45ml/ 2–3 tbsp egg, swirling to cover the base evenly. Cook until set. Repeat until all the mixture is used up.

3 Roll each pancake up and slice thinly into shreds. Set aside.

4 Bring the stock or consommé to the boil and add the pasta, breaking it up into short lengths. Cook for 3–5 minutes until the

pasta is almost tender, then add the chicken, and salt and pepper to taste. Heat through for about 2–3 minutes, then stir in the egg shreds. Serve immediately.

THAI CHICKEN SOUP

To make a Thai variation, use Chinese rice noodles instead of pasta. Stir 1.5ml/½ tsp dried lemon grass, 2 small whole fresh chillies and 60ml/4 tbsp coconut milk into the stock. Add 4 sliced spring onions and plenty of chopped fresh coriander.

Chinese-style Vegetable and Noodle Soup

This soup is wonderfully quick and easy to prepare.

Serves 4

1.2 litres/2 pints/5 cups vegetable or
   chicken stock

1 garlic clove, lightly crushed

2.5cm/1in piece fresh root ginger, peeled
   and cut into fine matchsticks

30ml/2 tbsp soy sauce

15ml/1 tbsp cider vinegar

75g/3oz fresh shiitake or button
   mushrooms, stalks removed and
   thinly sliced

2 large spring onions, thinly sliced on
   the diagonal

40g/1½oz vermicelli or other fine noodles

175g/6oz Chinese leaves, shredded

a few fresh coriander leaves

1 Pour the stock into a saucepan.
Add the garlic, root ginger, soy
sauce and vinegar. Bring to the
boil, then cover the pan and reduce
the heat to very low. Leave to
simmer gently for 10 minutes.
Remove the garlic clove from the
pan and discard.

2 Add the sliced mushrooms and
spring onions and bring the
soup back to the boil. Simmer for
5 minutes, uncovered, stirring
occasionally. Add the noodles and
shredded Chinese leaves. Simmer
for 3–4 minutes, or until the
noodles and vegetables are just
tender. Stir in the coriander leaves.
Simmer for a final 1 minute. Serve
the soup hot.

Seafood Wontons with Coriander Dressing

*These tasty wontons resemble
tortellini. Water chestnuts add a
light crunch to the filling.*

INGREDIENTS

Serves 4

225g/8oz cooked prawns, peeled
    and deveined
115g/4oz white crab meat
4 canned water chestnuts, finely diced
1 spring onion, finely chopped
1 small green chilli, seeded and
    finely chopped
1.5ml/¼ tsp grated fresh root ginger
1 egg, separated
20–24 wonton wrappers
salt and freshly ground black pepper
coriander leaves, to garnish

For the coriander dressing
30ml/2 tbsp rice vinegar
15ml/1 tbsp chopped, pickled ginger
90ml/6 tbsp olive oil
15ml/1 tbsp soy sauce
45ml/3 tbsp chopped coriander
30ml/2 tbsp finely diced red pepper

1 Finely dice the prawns and
place them in a bowl. Add the
crab meat, water chestnuts, spring
onion, chilli, ginger and egg white.
Season with salt and pepper to
taste and stir well.

2 Place a wonton wrapper on a
board. Put about 5ml/1 tsp of
the filling just above the centre of
the wrapper. With a pastry brush,
moisten the edges of the wrapper
with a little of the egg yolk. Bring
the bottom of the wrapper up over
the filling. Press gently to expel any
air, then seal the wrapper neatly in
a triangle.

3 For a more elaborate shape,
bring the two side points up
over the filling, overlap the points
and pinch the ends firmly together.
Space the filled wontons on a large
baking sheet lined with grease-
proof paper, so that they do not
stick together.

4 Half fill a large saucepan with
water. Bring to simmering
point. Add the filled wontons, a
few at a time, and simmer for
about 2–3 minutes, or until the
wontons float to the surface. When
ready, the wrappers will be translucent and the filling should be
cooked. Remove the wontons with
a large slotted spoon, drain them
briefly, then spread them on trays.
Keep warm while you cook the
remaining wontons.

5 Make the coriander dressing
by whisking all the ingredients
together in a bowl. Divide the
wontons among serving dishes,
drizzle with the dressing and serve,
garnished with a handful of
coriander leaves.

Spaghetti with Olives and Capers

This spicy sauce originated in the Naples area. It can be quickly assembled using a few store-cupboard ingredients.

INGREDIENTS

Serves 4

60ml/4 tbsp olive oil

2 garlic cloves, finely chopped

small piece of dried red chilli, crumbled

50g/2oz can anchovy fillets, chopped

350g/12oz tomatoes, fresh or
    canned, chopped

115g/4oz/1 cup stoned black olives

30ml/2 tbsp capers, rinsed

15ml/1 tbsp tomato purée

400g/14oz spaghetti

30ml/2 tbsp chopped fresh parsley

1 Heat the oil in a large frying pan. Add the garlic and the dried red chilli, and cook for 2–3 minutes until the garlic is just golden.

2 Add the chopped anchovies, and mash them into the garlic with a fork.

3 Add the fresh or canned tomatoes, olives, capers and tomato purée. Stir well and cook over a moderate heat.

4 Cook the spaghetti in plenty of boiling salted water until *al dente*. Drain well.

5 Turn the spaghetti into the sauce. Increase the heat and cook for 3–4 minutes, turning the pasta constantly. Sprinkle with parsley and serve at once.

Tagliolini with Asparagus

Tagliolini are very thin egg noodles, more delicate in texture than spaghetti. They go well with this subtle cream sauce, flavoured with fresh asparagus.

INGREDIENTS

Serves 4

450g/1lb fresh asparagus

egg pasta sheets made with 2 eggs, or
    350g/12oz fresh tagliolini or other
    egg noodles

50g/2oz/¼ cup butter

3 spring onions, finely chopped

3–4 fresh mint or basil leaves,
    finely chopped

150ml/¼ pint/⅔ cup double cream

50g/2oz/½ cup freshly grated
    Parmesan cheese

salt and ground black pepper

1 Peel the asparagus by inserting a small sharp knife at the base of the stalks and pulling upwards towards the tips. Drop them into a pan of boiling water and boil until just tender, about 4–6 minutes.

2 Remove from the pan, reserving the cooking water. Cut the tips off, and then cut the stalks into 4cm/1½in pieces. Set aside.

3 Make the egg pasta sheets, if using, and fold and cut into thin noodles, or feed through the narrowest setting of a pasta-making machine. Open them out and dry for 5–10 minutes.

4 Melt the butter in a large frying pan. Add the spring onions and herbs, and cook for 3–4 minutes. Stir in the cream and asparagus, and heat gently, but do not boil. Season to taste.

5 Bring the asparagus cooking water back to the boil. Add salt. Drop the noodles in all at once. Cook until just tender (freshly made noodles will cook in about 30–60 seconds). Drain thoroughly through a colander.

6 Turn the pasta into the pan with the sauce, increase the heat slightly and mix well. Stir in the Parmesan cheese. Mix well and serve at once.

Spaghetti Olio e Aglio

This is a classic recipe from Rome. Originally the food of the poor, involving nothing more than pasta, olive oil (olio) and garlic (aglio), this is a quick and filling dish which is fast becoming fashionable the world over.

INGREDIENTS

Serves 4

2 garlic cloves

30ml/2 tbsp roughly chopped
  fresh parsley

120ml/4fl oz/½ cup olive oil

450g/1lb spaghetti

salt and ground black pepper

1 Using a sharp knife, peel and finely chop the two cloves of garlic.

2 Using a nylon chopping board and a sharp knife, roughly chop the fresh parsley.

3 Heat the olive oil in a medium saucepan and add the garlic and a pinch of salt. Cook gently, stirring all the time, until golden. If the garlic becomes too brown, it will taste bitter and spoil the dish.

4 Meanwhile cook the spaghetti in plenty of boiling salted water according to the instructions on the packet until *al dente*. Drain well through a colander.

5 Toss with the warm – not sizzling – garlic and oil and add plenty of black pepper and the parsley. Serve immediately.

Orecchiette with Broccoli

Puglia, in southern Italy, specializes in imaginative pasta and vegetable combinations. Using the broccoli cooking water for boiling the pasta gives it more of the vegetable's lovely fresh flavour.

INGREDIENTS

Serves 6

800g/1¾lb broccoli

450g/1lb orecchiette or penne

90ml/6 tbsp olive oil

3 garlic cloves, finely chopped

6 anchovy fillets in oil

salt and ground black pepper

1 Peel the stems of the broccoli, starting from the base and pulling up towards the florets with a knife. Discard the woody parts of the stem. Cut the florets and stems into 5cm/2in pieces.

2 Bring a large pan of water to the boil. Drop in the broccoli and boil until barely tender, about 5–8 minutes. Remove the broccoli pieces from the pan to a serving bowl. Do not discard the broccoli cooking water.

3 Add salt to the broccoli cooking water and bring back to the boil. Drop in the pasta, stir well, and cook until *al dente*.

4 While the pasta is boiling, heat the oil in a small saucepan. Add the garlic and, after 2–3 minutes, the anchovy fillets. Using a fork, mash the anchovies and garlic to a smooth paste. Then cook for a further 3–4 minutes.

5 Before draining the pasta, ladle 1–2 cupfuls of the cooking water over the broccoli. Add the drained pasta and the hot anchovy and oil mixture. Mix well, and season with salt and pepper if necessary. Serve at once.

Spaghetti with Feta Cheese

We think of pasta as being essentially Italian but, in fact, the Greeks have a great appetite for it too. It complements tangy, full-flavoured feta cheese beautifully in this simple but effective dish.

INGREDIENTS

Serves 2–3

115g/4oz spaghetti
1 garlic clove
30ml/2 tbsp extra virgin olive oil
8 cherry tomatoes, halved
a little freshly grated nutmeg
salt and ground black pepper
75g/3oz feta cheese, crumbled
15ml/1 tbsp chopped fresh basil
a few black olives, to serve (optional)

1 Cook the spaghetti in plenty of boiling salted water according to the instructions on the packet, then drain well.

2 In the same pan gently heat the garlic clove in the olive oil for 1–2 minutes, then add the halved cherry tomatoes.

3 Increase the heat to fry the tomatoes lightly for 1 minute, then remove the garlic and discard.

4 Toss in the spaghetti, season with the nutmeg and salt and pepper to taste, then stir in the crumbled feta cheese and basil.

5 Check the seasoning, remembering that feta can be quite salty, and serve hot topped with black olives, if desired.

FISH &
MEAT DISHES

Linguine with Clam and Tomato Sauce

There are two types of traditional Italian clam sauce for pasta: one with tomatoes, as here, and another version without.

INGREDIENTS

Serves 4

900g/2lb fresh clams in the shell, or
   350g/12oz bottled clams, with
   their liquid
90ml/6 tbsp olive oil
1 garlic clove, crushed
400g/14oz tomatoes, fresh or canned, very
   finely chopped
350g/12oz linguine
60ml/4 tbsp chopped fresh parsley
salt and ground black pepper

1 Scrub and rinse the clams well under cold running water. Place them in a large saucepan with a cupful of water, and heat until the clams begin to open. Lift each clam out as soon as it opens, and scoop it out of its shell using a small spoon. Place in a bowl.

2 If the clams are large, chop them into 2 or 3 pieces. Reserve any liquid from the shells in a separate bowl. When all the clams have opened (discard any that do not open), pour the cooking liquid into the juices from the clams, and strain them through a piece of kitchen paper to remove any sand. If using bottled clams, use the liquid from the jar.

3 Place the olive oil in a medium saucepan with the garlic. Cook over a moderate heat until golden.

4 Remove the garlic and discard. Add the chopped tomatoes to the oil, and pour in the clam liquid. Mix well and cook over a low to moderate heat until the sauce begins to dry out and thickens slightly.

5 Cook the pasta in plenty of boiling salted water until just *al dente*, following the instructions on the packet.

6 A minute or two before the pasta is cooked, stir the parsley and the clams into the tomato sauce, and increase the heat. Add pepper and taste for seasoning, adding salt if necessary. Drain the pasta and turn into a serving dish. Pour on the hot sauce and mix well before serving immediately.

Farfalle with Prawns and Peas

A small amount of saffron in the sauce gives this dish a wonderful golden colour.

INGREDIENTS

Serves 4

45ml/3 tbsp olive oil

25g/1oz/2 tbsp butter

2 spring onions, chopped

350g/12oz/3 cups fresh or frozen
   peeled prawns

225g/8oz/1 cup frozen petit pois or
   peas, thawed

400g/14oz farfalle

250ml/8fl oz/1 cup dry white wine

a few saffron strands or pinch of
   powdered saffron

salt and ground black pepper

30ml/2 tbsp chopped fresh fennel or dill,
   to serve

1 Heat the oil and butter in a frying pan and sauté the spring onions lightly. Add the prawns and peas; cook for 2–3 minutes.

2 Cook the pasta in plenty of boiling salted water until just *al dente*.

3 Meanwhile, stir the wine and saffron into the prawn mixture.

4 Increase the heat and cook until the wine is reduced by about half. Add salt and pepper to taste. Cover and reduce the heat to low.

5 Drain the pasta and add it to the pan with the sauce. Stir over a high heat for 2–3 minutes, coating the pasta with the sauce. Sprinkle with the fresh herbs, and serve at once.

Short Pasta with Spring Vegetables

This colourful sauce makes the most of new crops of fresh, tender spring vegetables.

INGREDIENTS

Serves 6

1 or 2 small young carrots

2 spring onions

150g/5oz courgettes

2 tomatoes

75g/3oz/¾ cup shelled peas, fresh
   or frozen

75g/3oz fine green beans

1 yellow pepper

60ml/4 tbsp olive oil

25g/1oz/2 tbsp butter

1 garlic clove, finely chopped

5–6 fresh basil leaves, torn into pieces

500g/1¼lb short coloured or plain pasta,
   such as fusilli, penne or farfalle

salt and ground black pepper

freshly grated Parmesan cheese, to serve

1 Cut all the vegetables into small, bite-size pieces.

2 Heat the oil and butter in a large frying pan. Add the chopped vegetables, and cook over a moderate heat for 5–6 minutes, stirring occasionally. Add the garlic and the basil, and season with salt and pepper. Cover the pan and cook for a further 5–8 minutes, or until the vegetables are just tender.

3 Meanwhile, cook the pasta in plenty of boiling salted water until *al dente*. Before draining it, reserve a cupful of the pasta water.

4 Turn the pasta into the pan with the sauce, and mix well to distribute the vegetables. If the sauce seems too dry, add a few tablespoons of the reserved pasta water. Serve with the Parmesan handed round separately.

Noodles with Sausage and Spinach

Lap cheong are firm-textured, cured waxy pork sausages, available from Chinese food stores and supermarkets. They have an unusual sweet and savoury flavour.

INGREDIENTS

Serves 4

30ml/2 tbsp vegetable oil

115g/4oz rindless back bacon, cut into bite-size pieces

2 lap cheong, rinsed in warm water, drained and thinly sliced

2 garlic cloves, finely chopped

2 spring onions, roughly chopped

225g/8oz Chinese leaves or fresh spinach leaves, cut into 5cm/2in pieces

450g/1lb fresh Shanghai noodles

30ml/2 tbsp oyster sauce

30ml/2 tbsp soy sauce

freshly ground black pepper

1 Heat half the oil in a large wok or frying pan. Add the bacon and lap cheong, together with the garlic and spring onions. Stir-fry for a few minutes until golden. Using a slotted spoon, remove the mixture from the wok or frying pan and keep warm.

2 Add the remaining oil to the wok or pan. When hot, stir-fry the Chinese leaves or spinach over a high heat for about 3 minutes, until it just starts to wilt.

3 Add the noodles and return the lap cheong mixture to the wok or pan. Season with oyster sauce, soy sauce and pepper. Stir-fry until the noodles are heated through. Serve immediately.

Noodles with Sardines and Mustard

Serve this simple dish hot or at room temperature.

INGREDIENTS

Serves 4

350g/12oz broad egg noodles

60ml/4 tbsp olive oil

30ml/2 tbsp lemon juice

15ml/1 tbsp wholegrain mustard

1 garlic clove, finely chopped

225g/8oz ripe tomatoes, roughly chopped

1 small red onion, finely chopped

1 green pepper, seeded and finely diced

60ml/4 tbsp chopped fresh parsley

225g/8oz canned sardines, drained

salt and freshly ground black pepper

croûtons, made from 2 slices of bread, to serve (optional)

1 Cook the egg noodles in a large saucepan of boiling water for about 5–8 minutes, until they are just tender.

2 Meanwhile, to make the dressing, whisk together the olive oil, lemon juice, mustard and garlic in a small bowl with salt and pepper to taste.

3 Thoroughly drain the noodles, and tip them into a large serving bowl. Add the dressing and toss to coat well. Add the tomatoes, onion, green pepper, parsley and sardines and toss lightly again to mix. Season to taste with salt and pepper and serve with crisp croûtons, if using.

Seafood Spaghetti

This sauce offers a real, fresh seafood flavour. Serve with hunks of crusty French bread.

INGREDIENTS

INGREDIENTS

Serves 4

350g/12oz spaghetti

50g/2oz/¼ cup butter

1 onion, chopped

1 red pepper, cored, seeded and
coarsely chopped

2 garlic cloves, chopped

15ml/1 tbsp paprika

450g/1lb live mussels in the shell

150ml/¼ pint/⅔ cup dry white wine

30ml/2 tbsp chopped fresh parsley

225g/8oz/2 cups peeled prawns

150ml/¼ pint/⅔ cup crème fraîche

salt and ground black pepper

finely chopped fresh flat leaf parsley,
to garnish

1 Cook the pasta in plenty of boiling salted water according to the instructions on the packet.

2 Melt the butter in a frying pan and fry the onion, pepper, garlic and paprika for 5 minutes until almost softened.

3 Rinse and scrub the mussels, making sure all the shells are tightly shut or they close when tapped sharply with the back of a knife. Discard any open shells.

4 Add the wine to the pan and bring to the boil.

5 Stir in the mussels, parsley and prawns, cover and simmer for about 5 minutes until the mussels have opened. Discard any mussels that remain closed.

6 Using a slotted spoon, remove the shellfish from the pan and keep warm. Bring the juices back to the boil and boil rapidly until reduced by half.

7 Stir in the crème fraîche until well blended. Season to taste. Return the shellfish to the pan and simmer for 1 minute to heat them throughly.

8 Drain the pasta thoroughly and divide it among four serving plates. Spoon over the shellfish and serve, garnished with the finely chopped fresh flat leaf parsley.

Spaghetti alla Carbonara

It has been said that this dish was originally cooked by Italian coal miners or charcoal-burners, hence the name "carbonara". The secret of its creamy sauce is not to overcook the egg.

INGREDIENTS

Serves 4

175g/6oz unsmoked streaky bacon

1 garlic clove, chopped

3 eggs

450g/1lb spaghetti

60ml/4 tbsp freshly grated
   Parmesan cheese

salt and ground black pepper

1 Dice the bacon and place in a medium saucepan. Fry in its own fat with the garlic until brown. Keep warm until needed.

2 Whisk the eggs together in a mixing bowl.

3 Cook the spaghetti in plenty of boiling salted water according to the instructions on the packet or until *al dente*. Drain well.

4 Quickly turn the spaghetti into the pan with the bacon and stir in the eggs, a little salt, lots of pepper and half the cheese. Toss well to mix. The eggs should half-cook in the heat from the pasta. Serve in warmed bowls with the remaining Parmesan cheese sprinkled over each portion.

Tagliatelle with Hazelnut Pesto

Hazelnuts provide an interesting alternative to pine nuts in this delicious pesto sauce.

INGREDIENTS

Serves 4

2 garlic cloves, crushed

25g/1oz/1 cup fresh basil leaves

25g/1oz/¼ cup hazelnuts

200g/7oz/scant 1 cup skimmed milk soft cheese

225g/8oz dried tagliatelle, or 450g/1lb fresh

salt and ground black pepper

1 Place the garlic, basil, hazelnuts and cheese in a blender or food processor and process to form a thick paste.

2 Cook the tagliatelle in plenty of lightly salted boiling water according to the instructions on the packet until just tender, then drain thoroughly.

3 Spoon the sauce into the hot pasta, tossing until melted. Sprinkle with ground black pepper to taste and serve hot.

Spaghetti with Tuna Sauce

A speedy midweek meal, which can also be made with other pasta shapes, for a change.

INGREDIENTS

Serves 4

225g/8oz dried spaghetti, or 450g/1lb fresh

1 garlic clove, crushed

400g/14oz can chopped tomatoes

425g/15oz can tuna fish in brine, flaked

2.5ml/½ tsp chilli sauce (optional)

4 stoned black olives, chopped

salt and ground black pepper

1 Cook the spaghetti in plenty of lightly salted boiling water, according to the instructions on the packet, or until *al dente*. Drain well and keep hot until required.

2 Place the garlic and tomatoes in the saucepan and bring to the boil. Simmer, uncovered, for about 2–3 minutes.

3 Add the tuna, chilli sauce, if using, the olives and spaghetti. Heat well, add the seasoning to taste and serve hot.

COOK'S TIP

If fresh tuna is available, use 450g/1lb cut into small chunks, and add after step 2. Simmer for 6–8 minutes, then add the chilli, olives and pasta.

Fettuccine with Ham and Cream

Prosciutto is perfect for this rich and delicious dish, which makes a very elegant starter.

INGREDIENTS

Serves 4

115g/4oz prosciutto crudo or other
   unsmoked ham (raw or cooked)
50g/2oz/¼ cup butter
2 shallots, very finely chopped
150ml/¼ pint/⅔ cup double cream
350g/12oz fettucine
50g/2oz/½ cup grated Parmesan cheese
salt and ground black pepper
fresh parsley sprig, to garnish

1 Cut the fat from the ham and chop both lean and fat parts separately into small squares.

2 Melt the butter in a medium frying pan and add the shallots and the squares of ham fat. Cook until golden. Add the lean ham, and cook for a further 2 minutes. Season with black pepper. Stir in the cream, and keep warm over a low heat while the pasta is cooking.

3 Cook the pasta in plenty of boiling salted water until *al dente*. Drain, turn into a warmed serving dish and toss with the sauce. Stir in the cheese and serve immediately, garnished with a sprig of parsley.

Tagliatelle with Smoked Salmon

In Italy smoked salmon is imported and quite expensive. This elegant creamy sauce makes a little go a long way. Use a mixture of green and white pasta if you wish.

INGREDIENTS

Serves 4–5

175g/6oz smoked salmon slices or ends,
   fresh or frozen
300ml/½ pint/1¼ cups single cream
pinch of ground mace or grated nutmeg
350g/12oz green and white tagliatelle
salt and ground black pepper
45ml/3 tbsp snipped fresh chives,
   to garnish

1 Cut the salmon into thin strips about 5cm/2in long. Place in a bowl with the cream and the mace or nutmeg.

2 Cook the pasta in plenty of boiling salted water until it is just *al dente*.

3 Meanwhile, gently warm the cream and salmon mixture in a small saucepan, without boiling.

4 Drain the pasta, pour the sauce over and mix well. Season to taste and garnish with the chives.

Pasta Twists with Mushroom and Chorizo

The delicious combination of wild mushrooms and spicy sausage make this a tempting supper dish.

INGREDIENTS

Serves 4

350g/12oz pasta twists, such as cavatappi
60ml/4 tbsp olive oil
1 garlic clove, chopped
1 celery stick, chopped
225g/8oz chorizo sausage, sliced
225g/8oz mixed mushrooms, such as
    oyster, brown cap and shiitake
15ml/1 tbsp lemon juice
30ml/2 tbsp chopped fresh oregano
salt and ground black pepper
finely chopped fresh parsley, to garnish

1 Cook the pasta in plenty of boiling salted water according to the instructions on the packet.

2 Heat the oil in a frying pan and cook the garlic and celery for 5 minutes until the celery is softened but not browned.

> ### COOK'S TIP
> ∾
> This dish is delicious served with lashings of Parmesan cheese shavings. Use any combination of mushrooms for this flavoursome sauce.

3 Add the chorizo and cook for 5 minutes, stirring from time to time, until browned.

4 Add the mushrooms and cook for a further 4 minutes, stirring from time to time, until they are slightly softened.

5 Stir in the remaining ingredients, and heat through.

6 Drain the pasta thoroughly and turn into a serving dish. Toss with the sauce to coat. Serve immediately, garnished with finely chopped fresh parsley.

Spicy Beef Noodles

If you are hungry and only have a few minutes to spare for cooking, this colourful and healthy dish is an excellent choice.

INGREDIENTS

Serves 4

15ml/1 tbsp oil

450g/1lb/4 cups minced beef

2.5cm/1in piece fresh root ginger, sliced

5ml/1 tsp Chinese five-spice powder

1 red chilli, sliced

50g/2oz mange-touts

1 red pepper, seeded and chopped

1 carrot, sliced

115g/4oz beansprouts

15ml/1 tbsp sesame oil

cooked Chinese egg noodles, to serve

3 Add the mange-touts, the seeded and chopped red pepper and sliced carrot and cook for a further 3 minutes, stirring the mixture continuously.

4 Add the beansprouts and sesame oil and cook for a final 2 minutes. Serve immediately with Chinese egg noodles.

1 Heat the oil in a wok until almost smoking. Add the minced beef and cook for about 3 minutes, stirring all the time.

2 Add the ginger, Chinese five-spice powder and chilli. Cook for 1 minute.

Pasta with Devilled Kidneys

Ask your butcher to prepare the kidneys for you if you prefer.

INGREDIENTS

Serves 4

8–10 lambs' kidneys

15ml/1 tbsp sunflower oil

25g/1oz/2 tbsp butter

10ml/2 tsp paprika

5–10ml/1–2 tsp mild grainy mustard

salt, to taste

chopped fresh parsley, to garnish

225g/8oz fresh pasta, to serve

1 Cut the kidneys in half and neatly cut out the white cores with scissors. Cut the kidneys again if very large.

2 Heat the oil and butter together. Add the kidneys and cook, turning frequently, for about 2 minutes. Blend the paprika and mustard together with a little salt and stir into the pan.

3 Continue cooking the kidneys, basting frequently, for about a further 3–4 minutes.

4 Cook the pasta for about 10–12 minutes, or according to the instructions on the packet. Serve the kidneys and their sauce, topped with the chopped fresh parsley, and accompanied by the pasta.

Golden-topped Pasta

When it comes to the children helping you to plan the menus, this is the sort of dish that always wins hands down. It is also perfect for "padding out" if you have to feed eight instead of four people.

INGREDIENTS

Serves 4–6

225g/8oz dried pasta shells or spirals

115g/4oz/⅔ cup chopped cooked ham, beef or turkey

350g/12oz par-cooked mixed vegetables, such as carrots, cauliflower, beans, etc

a little oil

For the cheese sauce

25g/1oz/2 tbsp butter

25g/1oz/2 tbsp plain flour

300ml/½ pint/1¼ cups milk

175g/6oz/1½ cups grated Cheddar cheese

5–10ml/1–2 tsp mustard

salt and ground black pepper

1 Cook the pasta according to the instructions on the packet. Drain and place in a flameproof dish with the chopped meat, the vegetables and 5–10ml/1–2 tsp oil.

2 Melt the butter in a saucepan, stir in the flour and cook for 1 minute, stirring. Remove from the heat and gradually stir in the milk. Return to the heat, bring to the boil, stirring and cook for 2 minutes. Add half the cheese, the mustard and seasoning to taste.

3 Spoon the sauce over the meat and vegetables. Sprinkle with the rest of the cheese and grill quickly until golden and bubbling.

Short Pasta with Cauliflower

This is a pasta version of cauliflower cheese. The cauliflower water is used to cook the pasta.

INGREDIENTS

Serves 6

1 cauliflower

475ml/16fl oz/2 cups milk

1 bay leaf

50g/2oz/¼ cup butter

50g/2oz/½ cup flour

75g/3oz/¾ cup freshly grated Parmesan
    or Cheddar cheese

500g/1¼lb pennoni rigati or other
    short pasta

salt and ground black pepper

1 Bring a large pan of water to the boil. Wash the cauliflower well, and separate it into florets. Boil the florets until they are just tender, about 8–10 minutes.

Remove from the pan with a slotted spoon. Chop the cauliflower into bite-size pieces and set aside. Do not discard the cooking water in the pan.

2 Make a béchamel sauce by gently heating the milk with the bay leaf in a small saucepan. Do not let it boil. Melt the butter in a medium heavy-based saucepan. Add the flour, and mix in well with a wire whisk ensuring there are no lumps. Cook for 2–3 minutes, but do not let the butter burn.

3 Strain the hot milk into the flour and butter mixture all at once, and mix smoothly with the wire whisk.

4 Bring the sauce to the boil, stirring constantly, and cook for a further 4-5 minutes. Season to taste. Add the cheese, and stir over a low heat until melted. Stir in the cauliflower. Keep warm.

5 Bring the cauliflower cooking water back to the boil. Add salt, stir in the pasta and cook until *al dente*. Drain, and tip the pasta into a warmed serving dish. Pour over the sauce. Mix well, and serve at once.

Spaghetti with Bacon and Onion

This easy sauce is quickly made from ingredients that are almost always at hand.

INGREDIENTS

Serves 6

30ml/2 tbsp olive oil or lard

115g/4oz unsmoked streaky bacon, cut
    into matchsticks

1 small onion, finely chopped

120ml/4fl oz/½ cup dry white wine

450g/1lb tomatoes, fresh or
    canned, chopped

1.5ml/¼ tsp thyme leaves

600g/1lb 6oz spaghetti

salt and ground black pepper

freshly grated Parmesan cheese, to serve

1 In a medium frying pan, heat the oil or lard. Add the bacon and onion, and cook over a low to moderate heat until the onion is golden and the bacon has rendered its fat and is beginning to brown, about 8–10 minutes.

2 Add the wine to the bacon and onion, increase the heat and cook rapidly until the liquid boils off. Add the tomatoes, thyme, salt and pepper. Cover and cook over a moderate heat for 10–15 minutes.

3 Cook the pasta in plenty of boiling salted water until *al dente*. Drain, toss with the sauce and hand round the grated Parmesan cheese separately.

Spaghetti with Tomato Sauce

Don't be put off by the idea of anchovies, they give a wonderful richness to the sauce, without adding their usual salty flavour.

INGREDIENTS

Serves 4

45ml/3 tbsp olive oil

1 onion, chopped

1 large garlic clove, chopped

400g/14oz can of chopped tomatoes
    with herbs

60ml/4 tbsp dry white wine

350g/12oz dried spaghetti

5–10ml/1–2 tsp dark soft brown sugar

50g/2oz can anchovy fillets in oil

115g/4oz pepperoni sausage, chopped

15ml/1 tbsp chopped fresh basil

salt and ground black pepper

sprigs of basil, to garnish

1 Heat the oil in a saucepan and fry the onion and garlic for 2 minutes to soften. Add the tomatoes and wine, bring to the boil and leave to simmer gently for 10–15 minutes. Put the pasta on to cook as directed.

2 After the sauce has been cooking 10 minutes add the soft brown sugar and the anchovy fillets, drained and chopped. Mix well and cook for about a further 5 minutes or so.

3 Drain the pasta and toss in very little oil. Add to it the pepperoni and the basil and sprinkle with seasoning. Serve topped with the tomato sauce and garnish with the sprigs of basil.

Tortellini with Cheese Sauce

Here is a very quick way of making a delicious cheese sauce without all the usual effort. But do eat it when really hot before the sauce starts to thicken. Blue cheese would work just as well, for a change.

INGREDIENTS

Serves 4

450g/1lb fresh tortellini

115g/4oz/½ cup ricotta or cream cheese

60–90ml/4-6 tbsp milk

50g/2oz/½ cup St Paulin or mozzarella
    cheese, grated

50g/2oz/½ cup Parmesan cheese, grated

2 garlic cloves, crushed

30ml/2 tbsp chopped, mixed fresh herbs,
    such as parsley, chives, basil or oregano

salt and ground black pepper

1 Cook the pasta according to the packet instructions, in boiling, salted water, stirring occasionally.

2 Meanwhile, gently melt the ricotta or cream cheese with the milk in a large pan. When blended, stir in the St Paulin or mozzarella, half the Parmesan, and the garlic and herbs.

3 Drain the cooked pasta and add to the pan of sauce. Stir well, and allow to cook gently for 1–2 minutes so the cheeses melt well. Season to taste and serve with the remaining Parmesan cheese sprinkled on top.

VEGETARIAN
DISHES

Capellini with Rocket and Mange-touts

A light but filling pasta dish with the added pepperiness of fresh rocket leaves.

INGREDIENTS

Serves 4

250g/9oz capellini or angel hair pasta

225g/8oz mange-touts

75g/3oz rocket leaves

50g/2oz/¼ cup pine nuts, roasted

30ml/2 tbsp finely grated Parmesan cheese (optional)

30ml/2 tbsp olive oil (optional)

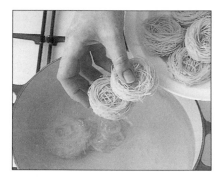

1 Cook the capellini or angel-hair pasta in plenty of boiling salted water, according to the instructions on the packet, until just *al dente*.

2 Meanwhile, carefully top and tail the mange-touts, and discard any that are damaged.

3 As soon as the pasta is cooked, drop in the rocket and mange-touts. Drain immediately.

4 Toss the pasta with the roasted pine nuts, and Parmesan and olive oil if using. Serve at once.

Pasta Salade Tiède

Boil a pan of pasta shapes and toss with vinaigrette dressing and some freshly prepared salad vegetables and you have the basis for a delicious warm salad.

INGREDIENTS

Serves 2

115g/4oz pasta shapes, such as shells

45ml/3 tbsp vinaigrette dressing

3 sun-dried tomatoes in oil, chopped

2 spring onions, sliced

25g/1oz watercress or rocket, chopped

¼ cucumber, halved, seeded and sliced

salt and ground black pepper

about 40g/1½oz pecorino cheese, coarsely grated, to garnish

1 Cook the pasta in plenty of boiling salted water according to the instructions on the packet. Drain and toss in the dressing.

2 Mix in the tomatoes, onions, watercress or rocket and cucumber. Season to taste.

3 Divide between two plates and sprinkle over the cheese. Serve at room temperature.

Penne with "Can-can" Sauce

The quality of canned pulses and tomatoes is so good that it is possible to transform them into a very fresh-tasting pasta sauce in minutes. Choose whatever pasta you like.

INGREDIENTS

Serves 3–4

225g/8oz penne

1 onion, sliced

1 red pepper, seeded and sliced

30ml/2 tbsp olive oil

400g/14oz chopped tomatoes

425g/15oz can chick-peas

30ml/2 tbsp dry vermouth (optional)

5ml/1 tsp dried oregano

1 large bay leaf

30ml/2 tbsp capers

salt and ground black pepper

1 Cook the pasta in plenty of boiling salted water according to the instructions on the packet, then drain. In a saucepan, gently fry the onion and pepper in the oil for about 5 minutes, stirring occasionally, until softened.

2 Add the tomatoes, chick-peas with their liquor, vermouth, if using, herbs and capers.

3 Season and bring to the boil, then simmer the mixture for about 10 minutes. Remove the bay leaf and mix in the pasta, reheat and serve hot.

Mushroom and Chilli Carbonara

*For a richer mushroom flavour, use
a small packet of dried Italian
porcini mushrooms in this quick
eggy sauce, and for an extra spicy
zing, toss in some chilli flakes too.*

INGREDIENTS

Serves 4

15g/½oz pack dried porcini mushrooms

300ml/½ pint/1¼ cups hot water

225g/8oz spaghetti

1 garlic clove, crushed

25g/1oz/2 tbsp butter

15ml/1 tbsp olive oil

225g/8oz button or chestnut mushrooms,
    thinly sliced

5ml/1 tsp dried red chilli flakes

2 eggs

300ml/½ pint/1¼ cups single cream

salt and ground black pepper

freshly grated Parmesan cheese and
    chopped fresh parsley, to serve

1 Soak the dried mushrooms in
the hot water for 15 minutes;
drain and reserve the liquor.

2 Cook the spaghetti according
to the instructions in plenty of
boiling salted water. Drain and
rinse in cold water.

3 In a large saucepan, lightly
sauté the garlic with the butter
and oil for half a minute.

4 Add the mushrooms,
including the soaked porcini
ones, and the chilli flakes, and stir
well. Cook for about 2 minutes.

5 Pour in the reserved soaking
liquor from the mushrooms
and boil the mixture to reduce
slightly.

6 Beat the eggs with the cream
and season well. Return the
cooked spaghetti to the pan and
toss in the eggs and cream. Reheat,
without boiling, and serve hot
sprinkled with grated Parmesan
cheese and chopped parsley.

VARIATION

Instead of mushrooms, try using
either finely sliced and sautéed
leeks or perhaps coarsely shredded
lettuce with peas. If chilli flakes are
too hot and spicy for you, then try
the delicious alternative of skinned
and chopped tomatoes with torn,
fresh basil leaves.

Tagliatelle with Sun-dried Tomatoes

Choose plain sun-dried tomatoes for this sauce, instead of those preserved in oil, if you wish to reduce the fat content of the dish.

INGREDIENTS

Serves 4

1 garlic clove, crushed

1 celery stick, finely sliced

115g/4oz/1 cup sun-dried tomatoes, finely chopped

90ml/3½fl oz/scant ½ cup red wine

8 plum tomatoes

350g/12oz dried tagliatelle

salt and ground black pepper

3 Add the plum tomatoes to the saucepan and simmer for a further 5 minutes. Season to taste.

4 Meanwhile, cook the tagliatelle in plenty of boiling salted water for 8–10 minutes, or until *al dente*. Drain well. Toss with half the sauce and serve on warmed plates, with the remaining sauce.

1 Put the garlic, celery, sun-dried tomatoes and wine into a large saucepan. Gently cook for about 15 minutes.

2 Slash the bottoms of the plum tomatoes and plunge into a saucepan of boiling water for 1 minute, then into a saucepan of cold water. Slip off their skins. Halve, remove the seeds and cores and roughly chop the flesh.

Fusilli with Mascarpone and Spinach

This creamy, green sauce tossed in lightly cooked pasta is best served with plenty of sun-dried tomato ciabatta bread.

INGREDIENTS

Serves 4

350g/12oz pasta spirals, such as fusilli
50g/2oz/¼ cup butter
1 onion, chopped
1 garlic clove, chopped
30ml/2 tbsp fresh thyme leaves
225g/8oz frozen spinach leaves, thawed
225g/8oz/1 cup mascarpone cheese
salt and ground black pepper
fresh thyme sprigs, to garnish

1 Cook the pasta in plenty of boiling salted water according to the instructions on the packet.

2 Melt the butter in a large saucepan and fry the onion for 10 minutes until softened.

3 Stir in the garlic, fresh thyme, spinach and seasoning and heat gently for about 5 minutes, stirring occasionally, until heated through.

4 Stir in the mascarpone cheese and cook gently until heated through. Do not boil.

5 Drain the pasta thoroughly and stir into the sauce. Toss until well coated. Serve immediately, garnished with fresh thyme.

COOK'S TIP

Mascarpone is a rich Italian cream cheese. If you cannot find any, use ordinary full-fat cream cheese instead.

Stir-fried Vegetables with Pasta

This is a colourful Chinese-style dish, easily prepared using pasta instead of Chinese noodles.

INGREDIENTS

Serves 4

1 carrot

175g/6oz small courgettes

175g/6oz runner or other green beans

175g/6oz baby sweetcorn

450g/1lb ribbon pasta, such as tagliatelle

salt, to taste

30ml/2 tbsp corn oil, plus extra for tossing the pasta

1cm/½in piece fresh root ginger, peeled and finely chopped

2 garlic cloves, finely chopped

90ml/6 tbsp yellow bean sauce

6 spring onions, sliced into 2.5cm/1in lengths

30ml/2 tbsp dry sherry

5ml/1 tsp sesame seeds, to garnish

1 Slice the carrot and courgettes diagonally into chunks. Slice the beans diagonally. Cut the baby sweetcorn diagonally in half.

2 Cook the pasta in plenty of boiling salted water according to the instructions on the packet. Drain, then rinse under hot water. Toss in a little corn oil.

3 Heat 30ml/2 tbsp oil until smoking in a wok or frying pan and add the ginger and garlic. Stir-fry for 30 seconds, then add the carrots, beans and courgettes.

4 Stir-fry for 3–4 minutes, then stir in the yellow bean sauce. Stir-fry for 2 minutes, add the spring onions, sherry and pasta and stir-fry for 1 minute or until piping hot. Sprinkle with sesame seeds and serve immediately.

Penne with Broccoli and Chilli

*For a milder flavour, remove the
seeds from the chilli.*

INGREDIENTS

Serves 4

350g/12oz penne

450g/1lb small broccoli florets

30ml/2 tbsp stock

1 garlic clove, crushed

1 small red chilli, sliced,
   or 2.5ml/½ tsp chilli sauce

60ml/4 tbsp natural low-fat yogurt

30ml/2 tbsp toasted pine nuts or
   cashew nuts

salt and ground black pepper

1 Add the pasta to a large pan of
lightly salted boiling water and
return to the boil. Then place the
broccoli in a steamer basket over
the top. Cover and cook for about
8–10 minutes until both are just
tender. Drain well.

2 Heat the stock and add the
crushed garlic and chilli or
chilli sauce. Stir over a low heat for
2–3 minutes.

3 Stir in the broccoli, pasta and
yogurt. Adjust the seasoning,
sprinkle with nuts and serve hot.

Tagliatelle with Spinach and Garlic Cheese

It's fun to mix ingredients from different cuisines and produce a delicious dish as a result. Italian pasta and spinach combine with Chinese soy sauce and French garlic-and-herb cream cheese to create this mouthwatering and wonderfully rich dish.

INGREDIENTS

Serves 4

225g/8oz tagliatelle, preferably
   mixed colours
225g/8oz fresh leaf spinach
30ml/2 tbsp light soy sauce
75g/3oz garlic-and-herb cheese
45ml/3 tbsp milk
salt and ground black pepper

1 Cook the tagliatelle in plenty of boiling salted water according to the instructions on the packet. Drain and return to the pan.

2 Blanch the spinach in a tiny amount of water until just wilted, then drain well, squeezing dry with the back of a wooden spoon. Chop roughly with scissors.

3 Return the spinach to its pan and stir in the soy sauce, garlic-and-herb cheese and milk. Bring slowly to the boil, stirring until smooth. Season to taste.

4 When the sauce is ready, pour over the pasta. Toss the pasta and sauce together and serve hot.

Linguine with Pesto Sauce

Pesto originates in Liguria, where the sea breezes are said to give the local basil a particularly fine flavour. It is traditionally made with a pestle and mortar, but it is easier to make in a food processor or blender. Freeze any spare pesto in an ice-cube tray for later use.

INGREDIENTS

Serves 5–6

65g/2½oz/¾ cup fresh basil leaves

3–4 cloves garlic, peeled

45ml/3 tbsp pine nuts

2.5ml/½ tsp salt

75ml/5 tbsp olive oil

50g/2oz/½ cup freshly grated
    Parmesan cheese

60ml/4 tbsp freshly grated
    pecorino cheese

ground black pepper

500g/1¼lb linguine

1 Place the basil, garlic, pine nuts, salt and olive oil in a blender or food processor and process until smooth. Remove to a bowl. If desired, the sauce may be frozen at this point, before the cheeses are added.

2 Stir in the cheeses (use all Parmesan if pecorino is not available). Taste for seasoning.

3 Cook the pasta in a large pan of rapidly boiling salted water until it is *al dente*. Just before draining, take about 60ml/4 tbsp of the cooking water and stir into the pesto sauce.

4 Drain the pasta thoroughly and toss it together with the sauce. Serve immediately.

Pasta Rapido with Parsley Pesto

Here is a fresh and lively sauce that will appeal to even the most jaded of appetites.

Serves 4

450g/1lb dried pasta, any shape
75g/3oz/³⁄₄ cup whole almonds
50g/2oz/¹⁄₂ cup flaked almonds
25g/1oz/¹⁄₄ cup freshly grated
   Parmesan cheese
pinch of salt

For the sauce

40g/1¹⁄₂oz fresh parsley
2 garlic cloves, crushed
45ml/3 tbsp olive oil
45ml/3 tbsp lemon juice
5ml/1 tsp sugar
250ml/8fl oz/1 cup boiling water

2 For the sauce, chop the parsley finely in a blender or food processor. Add the whole almonds; reduce to a fine consistency. Add the garlic, oil, lemon juice, sugar and water. Combine to a sauce.

3 Drain the pasta and combine with half the sauce. (The remainder of the sauce will keep in a screw-top jar in the fridge for up to ten days.) Top with Parmesan and flaked almonds.

1 Cook the pasta in plenty of boiling salted water, according to the instructions on the packet, until *al dente*. Toast the whole and flaked almonds separately under a moderate grill until golden brown. Set the flaked almonds aside.

Fusilli with Peppers and Onions

Peppers are characteristic of southern Italy. When grilled and peeled they have a delicious smoky flavour, and are easier to digest.

Serves 4

450g/1lb red and yellow peppers
90ml/6 tbsp olive oil
1 large red onion, thinly sliced
2 garlic cloves, minced
400g/14oz fusilli or other short pasta
45ml/3 tbsp finely chopped fresh parsley
salt and ground black pepper
freshly grated Parmesan cheese, to serve

1 Place the peppers under a hot grill and turn occasionally until they are blackened and blistered on all sides. Remove from the heat, place in a plastic bag, seal and leave for 5 minutes.

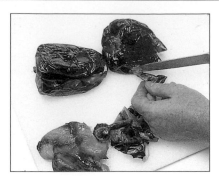

2 Peel the peppers. Cut them into quarters, remove the stems and seeds, and slice into thin strips.

3 Heat the oil in a large frying pan. Add the onion, and cook over a moderate heat until translucent, 5–8 minutes. Stir in the garlic, and cook for a further 2 minutes.

4 Cook the pasta in plenty of boiling salted water until just *al dente*. Do not drain yet.

5 Meanwhile, add the peppers to the onion, and mix together gently. Stir in about 45ml/3 tbsp of the pasta cooking water. Season with salt and pepper. Stir in the finely chopped fresh parsley.

6 Drain the pasta. Tip it into the pan with the vegetables, and cook over a moderate heat for 3–4 minutes, stirring constantly to mix the pasta into the sauce. Serve with the grated Parmesan cheese handed round separately.

Spaghetti with Fresh Tomato Sauce

The heat from the pasta will release the delicious flavours of this sauce. Only use the really red and soft tomatoes – large ripe beefsteak or Marmande tomatoes are ideal. Don't be tempted to use small hard tomatoes: they have very little flavour.

INGREDIENTS

Serves 4

4 large ripe tomatoes

2 garlic cloves, finely chopped

60ml/4 tbsp chopped fresh herbs, such as
    basil, marjoram, oregano or parsley

150ml/¼ pint/⅔ cup olive oil

450g/1lb spaghetti

salt and ground black pepper

1 Skin the tomatoes by placing in boiling water for 1 minute. Lift out with a slotted spoon and plunge into a bowl of cold water. Peel off the skins, then dry the tomatoes on kitchen paper.

2 Halve the tomatoes and squeeze out the seeds. Chop into 5mm/¼in cubes and mix with the garlic, herbs, olive oil and seasoning in a non-metallic bowl. Cover and allow the flavours to mellow for at least 30 minutes.

3 Cook the pasta in plenty of boiling salted water, according to the instructions on the packet.

4 Drain the pasta and mix with the sauce. Cover with a lid and leave for 2–3 minutes, then toss again and serve immediately.

VARIATION

Mix 115g/4oz/1 cup stoned and chopped black Greek olives into the sauce just before serving.

Pasta Shells with Tomatoes and Rocket

This pretty coloured pasta dish relies for its success on the salad green, rocket. Available in large supermarkets, it is a leaf easily grown in the garden or a window-box and tastes slightly peppery.

INGREDIENTS

Serves 4

450g/1lb pasta shells

450g/1lb ripe cherry tomatoes

75g/3oz fresh rocket leaves

45ml/3 tbsp olive oil

salt and ground black pepper

Parmesan cheese shavings, to serve

1 Cook the pasta in plenty of boiling salted water according to the instructions on the packet, until *al dente*. Drain well.

2 Halve the tomatoes. Trim, wash and dry the rocket leaves.

3 Heat the oil in a large saucepan, add the tomatoes and cook for barely 1 minute. The tomatoes should only just heat through and not disintegrate.

4 Add the pasta, then the rocket. Carefully stir to mix and heat through. Season well with salt and ground black pepper. Serve immediately with plenty of Parmesan cheese shavings.

Pasta Bows with Fennel and Walnut

A scrumptious blend of walnuts and crisp steamed fennel.

INGREDIENTS

Serves 4

75g/3oz/½ cup walnuts, roughly chopped

1 garlic clove, chopped

25g/1oz fresh flat-leaf parsley, picked
  from the stalks

115g/4oz/½ cup ricotta cheese

450g/1lb pasta bows

450g/1lb fennel bulbs

chopped walnuts, to garnish

1 Place the chopped walnuts, garlic and parsley in a food processor. Pulse until roughly chopped. Transfer to a bowl and stir in the ricotta cheese.

2 Cook the pasta following the instructions on the packet until *al dente*. Drain thoroughly.

3 Slice the fennel thinly and steam for 4–5 minutes until just tender but still crisp.

4 Return the pasta to the pan and add the walnut mixture and the fennel. Toss well and sprinkle with the chopped walnuts to garnish. Serve immediately.

Pasta with Spring Vegetables

Don't be tempted to use dried herbs in this flavoursome dish.

Serves 4

115g/4oz broccoli florets

115g/4oz baby leeks

225g/8oz asparagus

1 small fennel bulb

115g/4oz/1 cup fresh or frozen peas

40g/1½oz/3 tbsp butter

1 shallot, chopped

45ml/3 tbsp chopped fresh mixed herbs, such as parsley, thyme and sage

300ml/½ pint/1¼ cups double cream

350g/12oz dried penne

salt and ground black pepper

freshly grated Parmesan cheese, to serve

1 Divide the broccoli florets into tiny sprigs. Cut the leeks and asparagus diagonally into 5cm/2in lengths. Trim the fennel bulb and remove any tough outer leaves. Cut into wedges, leaving the layers attached at the root ends so the pieces stay intact.

2 Cook each vegetable, including the peas, separately in boiling salted water until just tender – use the same water for each vegetable. Drain well and keep warm.

3 Melt the butter in a separate pan, add the chopped shallot and cook, stirring occasionally, until softened but not browned. Stir in the herbs and cream and cook for a few minutes, until slightly thickened.

4 Meanwhile, cook the pasta in plenty of boiling salted water for 10 minutes until *al dente*. Drain well and add to the sauce with the vegetables. Toss gently and season with plenty of pepper.

5 Serve the pasta hot with a sprinkling of freshly grated Parmesan cheese.

Fettuccine all'Alfredo

A classic dish from Rome, Fettuccine all'Alfredo is simply pasta tossed with double cream, butter and freshly grated Parmesan cheese. Popular additions are peas and strips of ham.

INGREDIENTS

Serves 4

25g/1oz/2 tbsp butter

150ml/¼ pint/⅔ cup double cream, plus
    60ml/4 tbsp extra

450g/1lb fettuccine

50g/2oz/½ cup freshly grated Parmesan
    cheese, plus extra to serve

freshly grated nutmeg

salt and ground black pepper

1 Place the butter and 150ml/ ¼ pint/⅔ cup of the cream in a heavy saucepan, bring to the boil and simmer for 1 minute until slightly thickened.

2 Cook the fettuccine in plenty of boiling salted water according to the instructions on the packet, but for 2 minutes less time, until *al dente*.

3 Drain very well and turn into the pan with the cream sauce.

4 Place on the heat and turn the pasta in the sauce to coat thoroughly.

5 Add the extra 60ml/4 tbsp cream, the cheese, salt and pepper to taste and a little grated nutmeg. Toss until well coated and heated through. Serve at once with extra grated Parmesan cheese.

Paglia e Fieno

The title of this dish translates as "straw and hay" which refers to the yellow and green colours of the pasta when mixed together. Fresh peas make all the difference to this dish.

INGREDIENTS

Serves 4

50g/2oz/4 tbsp butter

350g/12oz/3 cups frozen petits pois or
   900g/2lb fresh peas, shelled

150ml/¼ pint/⅔ cup double cream, plus
   60ml/4 tbsp extra

450g/1lb tagliatelle (plain and
   green mixed)

50g/2oz/½ cup freshly grated Parmesan
   cheese, plus extra to serve

freshly grated nutmeg

salt and ground black pepper

1 Melt the butter in a heavy saucepan and add the peas. Sauté for 2–3 minutes, then add the cream, bring to the boil and simmer for 1 minute until the mixture is slightly thickened.

2 Cook the plain and green mixed tagliatelle in plenty of boiling salted water according to the instructions on the packet, but for 2 minutes less time, until it is just *al dente*. Drain well and then turn into the saucepan containing the cream and pea sauce.

3 Place on the heat and turn the pasta in the sauce to coat. Pour in the extra cream, the cheese, salt and pepper to taste and a little grated nutmeg. Toss until well coated and heated through. Serve immediately with extra freshly grated Parmesan cheese.

COOK'S TIP

Sautéed mushrooms and narrow strips of cooked ham also make good additions to this dish.

Tagliatelle with "Hit-the-pan" Salsa

It is possible to make a hot, filling meal within just 15 minutes with this quick-cook salsa sauce. If you have no time don't peel the tomatoes.

INGREDIENTS

Serves 2

115g/4oz tagliatelle

45ml/3 tbsp olive oil, preferably extra virgin

3 large tomatoes

1 garlic clove, crushed

4 spring onions, sliced

1 green chilli, halved, seeded and sliced

juice of 1 orange (optional)

30ml/2 tbsp chopped fresh parsley

salt and ground black pepper

grated cheese, to serve (optional)

1 Cook the tagliatelle in plenty of boiling salted water until *al dente*. Drain and toss in a little of the oil. Season well.

2 Skin the tomatoes by dipping them in a bowl of boiling water for about 45 seconds and then into cold water. The skins should slip off easily. Roughly chop the flesh.

3 Heat the remaining oil until quite hot and stir-fry the garlic, onions and chilli for 1 minute.

4 Add the tomatoes, orange juice, if using, and parsley. Season well and stir in the tagliatelle to reheat. Serve with grated cheese, if desired.

COOK'S TIP

You could use any pasta shape for this recipe. It would be particularly good with large rigatoni or linguini, or as a sauce for fresh ravioli or tortellini.

SPECIAL
OCCASION
DISHES

~

Tagliatelle with Saffron Mussels

Mussels in a saffron and cream sauce are served with tagliatelle in this recipe, but you can use any other pasta if you prefer.

INGREDIENTS

Serves 4

1.75kg/4–4½lb live mussels in the shell

150ml/¼ pint/⅔ cup dry white wine

2 shallots, chopped

350g/12oz dried tagliatelle

25g/1oz/2 tbsp butter

2 garlic cloves, crushed

250ml/8fl oz/1 cup double cream

generous pinch of saffron strands

1 egg yolk

salt and ground black pepper

30ml/2 tbsp chopped fresh parsley,
   to garnish

1 Scrub the mussels well under cold running water. Remove the "beards" and discard any mussels that are open.

2 Place the mussels in a large pan with the wine and shallots. Cover and cook over a high heat, shaking the pan occasionally, for 5-8 minutes until the mussels have opened. Drain the mussels, reserving the liquid. Discard any that remain closed. Shell all but a few of the mussels and keep warm.

3 Bring the reserved cooking liquid to the boil, then reduce by half. Strain into a jug to remove any grit.

4 Cook the tagliatelle in plenty of boiling salted water for about 10 minutes, until *al dente*.

5 Meanwhile, melt the butter and fry the garlic for 1 minute. Pour in the mussel liquid, cream and saffron strands. Heat gently until the sauce thickens slightly. Off the heat, stir in the egg yolk, shelled mussels, and season.

6 Drain the tagliatelle and transfer to warmed serving bowls. Spoon the sauce over and sprinkle with chopped parsley. Garnish with the mussels in shells and serve at once.

Tortellini with Mushrooms and Cheese

You can use any type of mushroom in this sauce. Wild mushrooms would be delicious, but might be expensive. You could use a mixture of wild and cultivated mushrooms.

INGREDIENTS

Serves 4

450g/1lb ricotta and spinach-
    filled tortellini
50g/2oz/¼ cup butter
2 garlic cloves, chopped
225g/8oz/3 cups sliced mushrooms
15g/½oz/1 tbsp plain flour
175ml/6fl oz/¾ cup milk
50g/2oz/⅔ cup grated Parmesan cheese
50g/2oz/½ cup grated fontina cheese
100g/4oz/⅔ cup ricotta cheese
60ml/4 tbsp single cream
30ml/2 tbsp snipped fresh chives
salt and freshly ground black pepper

1 Cook the pasta in plenty of salted boiling water according to the packet instructions.

2 Melt the butter in a large, heavy-based frying pan. Add the garlic and mushrooms and fry, stirring frequently, for about 5 minutes, until browned.

3 Remove the mushrooms from the pan and take the pan off the heat. Stir the flour into the pan, then stir in the milk until it has been absorbed by the flour.

4 Return the pan to the heat and stir in the Parmesan, fontina and ricotta cheeses and bring the mixture to just below boiling point. Add the cream and chives and season to taste. Return the mushrooms to the pan and gently heat through.

5 Drain the pasta and transfer to a large, warm serving bowl. Pour over the sauce and toss to coat. Serve immediately.

COOK'S TIP
~

Italians would probably use porcini mushrooms, also known as ceps, because of their strong flavour and firm texture when cooked. If you cannot find fresh porcini, try the dried variety.

Pasta Rounds with Parmesan Sauce

This is an extremely quick and simple sauce, but very tasty – perfect for hungry people in a hurry.

INGREDIENTS

Serves 4

450g/1lb pasta rounds (castiglioni)
50g/2oz/¼ cup butter
300ml/½ pint/1¼ cups double cream
175g/6oz/2 cups freshly grated
    Parmesan cheese
30ml/2 tbsp pine nuts, toasted
salt and freshly ground black pepper
chopped fresh flat leaf parsley, to garnish

1 Cook the pasta in plenty of salted boiling water according to the packet instructions.

2 Heat the butter and cream together in a saucepan over a low heat, but do not allow the mixture to boil.

3 Stir in half the Parmesan cheese and heat gently, stirring occasionally. Keep the sauce warm.

4 Drain the pasta and transfer to a warm serving bowl. Stir in the remaining Parmesan cheese and season to taste. Pour over the sauce and toss. Sprinkle on the pine nuts and garnish with parsley.

Tagliatelle with Prosciutto and Parmesan

This is a really simple dish, prepared in minutes from the best ingredients.

INGREDIENTS

Serves 4

115g/4oz prosciutto

450g/1lb tagliatelle

75g/3oz/6 tbsp butter

50g/2oz/½ cup freshly grated
    Parmesan cheese

salt and ground black pepper

a few fresh sage leaves, to garnish

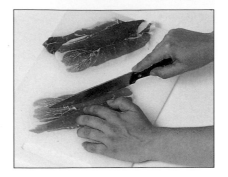

1 Cut the prosciutto into strips the same width as the tagliatelle. Cook the pasta in plenty of boiling salted water according to the instructions on the packet.

2 Meanwhile, melt the butter gently in a saucepan, stir in the prosciutto strips and heat through over a very gentle heat, being careful not to fry.

3 Drain the tagliatelle through a colander and pile into a warmed serving dish.

4 Sprinkle over all the Parmesan cheese and pour over the buttery prosciutto. Season well with black pepper and garnish with the sage leaves.

Spaghetti with Clams

Try chopped fresh dill for a delicious alternative in this dish.

Serves 4

24 live clams in the shell, scrubbed
250ml/8fl oz/1 cup water
120ml/4fl oz/½ cup dry white wine
450g/1lb spaghetti, preferably Italian
75ml/5 tbsp olive oil
2 garlic cloves, minced
45ml/3 tbsp chopped fresh parsley
salt and ground black pepper

1 Rinse the clams well in cold water and drain. Place in a large saucepan with the water and wine and bring to the boil. Cover and steam until the shells open, about 6–8 minutes.

2 Discard any clams that have not opened. Remove the clams from their shells. If large, chop them roughly.

3 Strain the cooking liquid through a strainer lined with muslin. Place in a small saucepan and boil rapidly until reduced by about half. Set aside.

4 Cook the spaghetti in plenty of boiling salted water according to the instructions on the packet until *al dente*.

5 Meanwhile, heat the olive oil in a large frying pan. Add the garlic and cook for 2–3 minutes, but do not let it brown. Add the reduced clam liquid and the parsley. Cook over a low heat until the spaghetti is ready.

6 Drain the spaghetti. Add to the frying pan, increase the heat to medium, and add the clams. Cook for 3–4 minutes, stirring, to coat the spaghetti with the sauce and to heat the clams.

7 Season with salt and pepper and serve at once.

Pasta Bows with Smoked Salmon and Dill

In Italy, pasta cooked with smoked salmon is very fashionable. This is a quick and luxurious sauce.

INGREDIENTS

Serves 4

6 spring onions

50g/2oz/4 tbsp butter

90ml/6 tbsp dry white wine or vermouth

450ml/¾ pint/1¾ cups double cream

freshly grated nutmeg

225g/8oz smoked salmon

30ml/2 tbsp chopped fresh dill or
    15ml/1 tbsp dried

freshly squeezed lemon juice

450g/1lb farfalle

salt and ground black pepper

1 Slice the spring onions finely. Melt the butter in a saucepan and gently fry the spring onions for 1 minute until softened.

2 Add the wine or vermouth and boil hard to reduce to about 30ml/2 tbsp. Stir in the cream and add salt, pepper and nutmeg to taste. Bring to the boil and simmer for 2–3 minutes until the sauce is slightly thickened.

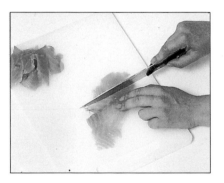

3 Cut the smoked salmon into 2.5cm/1in squares and stir into the sauce with the dill. Taste and add a little lemon juice. Keep the sauce warm.

4 Cook the pasta in plenty of boiling salted water according to the instructions on the packet. Drain well. Toss the pasta with the sauce and serve immediately.

Pasta Tossed with Grilled Vegetables

A hearty dish to be eaten with crusty bread and washed down with a robust red wine. Try barbecuing the vegetables for a really smoky flavour.

INGREDIENTS

Serves 4

1 aubergine

2 courgettes

1 red pepper

3 garlic cloves, unpeeled

about 150ml/¼ pint/⅔ cup good olive oil

450g/1lb ribbon pasta pappardelle

salt and ground black pepper

a few sprigs fresh thyme, to garnish

1 Preheat the grill. With a sharp knife, slice the aubergine and courgettes lengthways.

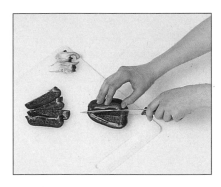

2 Halve the pepper, cut out the stalk and white pith and scrape out the seeds. Slice the pepper lengthways into eight pieces.

3 Line a grill pan with foil and arrange the vegetables and unpeeled garlic in a single layer over the foil. Brush liberally with oil and season with salt and ground black pepper.

4 Grill until slightly charred, turning once. If necessary, cook the vegetables in two batches.

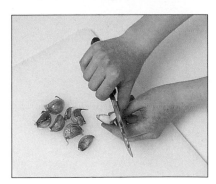

5 Cool the garlic, remove the charred skins and halve. Toss the vegetables with olive oil and keep warm.

6 Meanwhile cook the pasta in plenty of boiling salted water according to the instructions on the packet. Drain well and toss with the grilled vegetables. Serve immediately garnished with sprigs of fresh thyme.

Spinach and Ricotta Conchiglie

Large pasta shells are designed to hold a variety of delicious stuffings. Few are more pleasing than this mixture of spinach and ricotta.

INGREDIENTS

Serves 4

350g/12oz large conchiglie

450ml/¾ pint/1¾ cups passata or
    tomato pulp

275g/10oz frozen chopped
    spinach, thawed

50g/2oz crustless white bread, crumbled

120ml/4fl oz/½ cup milk

45ml/3 tbsp olive oil

250g/9oz ricotta cheese

pinch of grated nutmeg

1 garlic clove, crushed

15ml/1 tsbp olive oil

2.5ml/½ tsp black olive paste (optional)

25g/1oz/2 tbsp pine nuts

Parmesan cheese, for sprinkling

salt and ground black pepper

1 Cook the pasta in plenty of boiling salted water according to the instructions on the packet. Rinse under cold water, drain and reserve until needed.

2 Pour the passata or tomato pulp into a nylon sieve over a bowl and strain to thicken. Place the spinach in another sieve and press out any excess liquid with the back of a spoon.

3 Place the bread, milk and oil in a blender or food processor and process to combine. Add the spinach and ricotta cheese and season with salt, pepper and grated nutmeg.

4 Combine the passata or tomato pulp with the garlic, olive oil and olive paste, if using. Spread the sauce evenly over the base of an ovenproof dish.

5 Spoon the spinach mixture into a piping bag fitted with a large plain nozzle and fill the pasta shapes (alternatively fill with a spoon). Arrange the pasta shapes over the sauce.

6 Preheat the grill to a moderate heat. Heat the pasta through in the microwave on a high power for 4 minutes. Scatter with Parmesan cheese and pine nuts, and finish under the grill to brown the cheese until bubbling.

Pappardelle with Beans and Mushrooms

A mixture of wild and cultivated mushrooms help to give this dish a rich and nutty flavour.

INGREDIENTS

Serves 4

30ml/2 tbsp olive oil

50g/2oz/4 tbsp butter

2 shallots, chopped

2–3 garlic cloves, crushed

675g/1½lb mixed mushrooms, thickly sliced

4 sun-dried tomatoes in oil, drained and chopped

90ml/6 tbsp dry white wine

400g/14oz can borlotti beans, drained

45ml/3 tbsp grated Parmesan cheese

30ml/2 tbsp chopped fresh parsley

salt and ground black pepper

cooked pappardelle, to serve

1 Heat the oil and butter in a frying pan and fry the shallots until they are soft.

2 Add the garlic and mushrooms and fry for 3–4 minutes. Stir in the sun-dried tomatoes, wine and add seasoning to taste.

3 Stir in the borlotti beans and cook for 5–6 minutes, until most of the liquid has evaporated from the pan and the beans are warmed through.

4 Stir in the grated Parmesan cheese. Sprinkle with parsley and serve immediately with freshly cooked pappardelle.

Curly Spaghetti with Walnut and Cream

A classic Italian dish with a strong, nutty flavour, this should be served with a delicately flavoured salad.

INGREDIENTS

Serves 4

350g/12oz curly spaghetti (fusilli col buco)

50g/2oz/½ cup walnut pieces

25g/1oz/2 tbsp butter

300ml/½ pint/1¼ cups milk

50g/2oz/1 cup fresh breadcrumbs

25g/1oz/2 tbsp freshly grated Parmesan cheese

pinch of freshly grated nutmeg

salt and ground black pepper

fresh rosemary sprigs, to garnish

1 Cook the pasta in plenty of boiling salted water according to the instructions on the packet. Meanwhile, preheat the grill.

2 Spread the walnuts evenly over the grill pan. Grill for about 5 minutes, turning occasionally until evenly toasted.

3 Remove the walnuts from the heat, place in a clean dish towel and rub away the skins. Roughly chop the nuts.

4 Heat the butter and milk in a saucepan until the butter is completely melted.

5 Stir in the breadcrumbs and nuts and heat gently for 2 minutes, stirring constantly until thickened.

6 Add the Parmesan cheese, nutmeg and seasoning to taste.

7 Drain the pasta thoroughly through a colander and toss in the sauce. Serve immediately, garnished with fresh sprigs of rosemary.

Tagliatelle with Cheese and Asparagus Sauce

This attractive sauce is best served with a leafy red salad.

Serves 4

225g/8oz asparagus tips
350g/12oz tagliatelle
115g/4oz/½ cup butter
1 onion, chopped
1 garlic clove, chopped
30ml/2 tbsp chicken stock or water
150ml/¼ pint/⅔ cup double cream
75g/3oz/¾ cup grated mozzarella cheese
salt and freshly ground black pepper
fresh flat leaf parsley sprigs, to garnish

3 Melt the butter in a large frying pan, add the onion and fry over a medium heat for 5 minutes, until soft and translucent.

6 Add the mozzarella cheese and simmer for a further minute. Season the sauce to taste with salt and pepper.

1 Plunge the asparagus into a pan of boiling salted water and cook for 5–10 minutes, until tender. Drain thoroughly.

2 Cook the pasta in plenty of salted boiling water according to the packet instructions.

4 Stir in the asparagus, garlic and chicken stock or water.

5 Stir in the cream and bring to the boil. Lower the heat and simmer, stirring occasionally, for 2 minutes.

7 Drain the pasta thoroughly and transfer to a large, warm serving dish. Pour over the sauce and toss well to coat. Garnish with the flat leaf parsley sprigs and serve immediately.

COOK'S TIP

You can use either the thin green variety or the pale, fat blanched type of asparagus for this dish. Whichever type you choose, when you are buying it, make sure the buds are tight and the spears are firm, unwrinkled and evenly coloured. Do not discard the tough part of the stalks, as they can be used to make a delicately flavoured vegetable stock.

SALADS

Wholemeal Pasta Salad

This substantial vegetarian salad is easily assembled from any combination of seasonal vegetables. Use raw or lightly blanched vegetables, or a mixture of both.

INGREDIENTS

Serves 8

450g/1lb short wholemeal pasta, such as
　fusilli or penne
45ml/3 tbsp olive oil
2 carrots
1 small bunch broccoli
175g/6oz/1½ cups shelled peas, fresh
　or frozen
1 red or yellow pepper
2 celery sticks
4 spring onions
1 large tomato
75g/3oz/¾ cup stoned olives
115g/4oz/1 cup diced Cheddar or
　mozzarella cheese or a combination
　of both
salt and ground black pepper

For the dressing
45ml/3 tbsp white wine or
　balsamic vinegar
60ml/4 tbsp olive oil
15ml/1 tbsp Dijon mustard
15ml/1 tbsp sesame seeds
10ml/2 tsp chopped mixed fresh herbs,
　such as parsley, thyme and basil

1 Cook the pasta in plenty of boiling salted water until *al dente*. Drain, and rinse under cold water to stop the cooking. Drain well and turn into a large bowl. Toss with 45ml/3 tbsp of the olive oil and set aside. Allow the pasta to cool completely.

2 Lightly blanch the carrots, broccoli and peas in a large pan of boiling water. Refresh under cold water. Drain well.

3 Chop the carrots and broccoli into bite-size pieces and add to the pasta with the peas. Slice the pepper, celery, spring onions and tomato into small pieces. Add them to the salad with the olives.

4 Make the dressing in a small bowl by combining the vinegar with the oil and mustard. Stir in the sesame seeds and herbs. Mix the dressing into the salad. Taste for seasoning, adding salt, pepper or more olive oil and vinegar if necessary. Stir in the cheese, then allow the salad to stand for about 15 minutes before serving.

Pasta, Asparagus and Potato Salad

A meal in itself, this is a real treat when made with fresh asparagus just in season.

INGREDIENTS

Serves 4

225g/8oz wholemeal pasta shapes
60ml/4 tbsp extra virgin olive oil
350g/12oz baby new potatoes
225g/8oz fresh asparagus
115g/4oz Parmesan cheese
salt and ground black pepper

1 Cook the pasta in boiling salted water according to the instructions on the packet. Drain well and toss with the olive oil and salt and pepper while still warm.

2 Wash the potatoes and cook in boiling salted water for about 12–15 minutes or until tender. Drain and toss with the pasta.

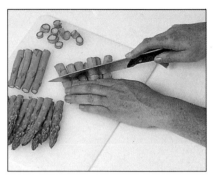

3 Trim any woody ends off the asparagus and halve the stalks if very long. Blanch in boiling salted water for 6 minutes until bright green and still crunchy. Drain, refresh in cold water and allow to cool. Drain and pat dry.

4 Toss the asparagus with the potatoes and pasta, season and transfer to a shallow bowl. Using a rotary vegetable peeler, shave over the Parmesan. Serve immediately.

Warm Pasta Salad with Ham and Egg

In the summer months when the weather is hot, try serving your pasta calda, *as a warm salad. Here it is served with ham, eggs and asparagus. A mustard dressing made from the thick part of asparagus provides a rich accompaniment.*

INGREDIENTS

Serves 4

450g/1lb asparagus

salt, to taste

450g/1lb dried tagliatelle

225g/8oz sliced cooked ham, 5mm/¼in
thick, cut into fingers

2 eggs, hard-boiled and sliced

50g/2oz Parmesan cheese, shaved

For the dressing

50g/2oz cooked potato

75g/5 tbsp olive oil, preferably Sicilian

15ml/1 tbsp lemon juice

10ml/2 tsp Dijon mustard

120ml/4fl oz/½ cup vegetable stock

1 Bring a saucepan of salted water to the boil. Trim and discard the tough woody parts of the asparagus. Cut the asparagus in half and boil the thicker halves for 12 minutes. After 6 minutes throw in the tips. Refresh under cold water until warm, then drain.

2 Finely chop 150g/5oz of the asparagus middle section. Place in a blender or food processor with the dressing ingredients and process until smooth. Season to taste with salt and pepper.

3 Cook the pasta in plenty of boiling salted water according to the instructions on the packet. Refresh under cold water until warm, then drain. Dress with the asparagus sauce and turn out on to four pasta plates. Top the pasta with the ham, hard-boiled eggs and asparagus tips. Finish with Parmesan cheese shavings.

Mediterranean Salad with Basil

A type of Salade Niçoise with pasta, conjuring up all the sunny flavours of the Mediterranean.

INGREDIENTS

Serves 4

225g/8oz chunky pasta shapes
175g/6oz fine green beans
2 large ripe tomatoes
50g/2oz fresh basil leaves
200g/7oz can tuna fish in oil, drained
2 hard-boiled eggs, shelled and sliced
   or quartered
50g/2oz can anchovy fillets, drained
capers and black olives

For the dressing

90ml/6 tbsp extra virgin olive oil
30ml/2 tbsp white wine vinegar or
   lemon juice
2 garlic cloves, crushed
2.5ml/½ tsp Dijon mustard
30ml/2 tbsp chopped fresh basil
salt and ground black pepper

1 Whisk all the ingredients for the dressing together and leave to infuse while you make the salad.

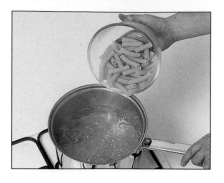

2 Cook the pasta in plenty of boiling salted water according to the instructions on the packet. Drain well and cool.

3 Trim the beans and blanch in boiling salted water for about 3 minutes. Drain and refresh in cold water.

4 Slice or quarter the tomatoes and arrange in the base of a bowl. Moisten with a little dressing and cover with a quarter of the basil leaves. Then cover with the beans. Moisten with a little more dressing and cover with a third of the remaining basil.

5 Cover with the pasta tossed in a little more dressing and half the remaining basil. Roughly flake the tuna, then add to the bowl.

6 Arrange the eggs on top, then finally scatter over the anchovy fillets, capers and black olives. Pour over the remaining dressing and garnish with the remaining basil. Serve immediately. Don't be tempted to chill this salad – all the flavour will be dulled.

Roquefort and Walnut Pasta Salad

This is a simple earthy salad, relying totally on the quality of the ingredients. There is no real substitute for Roquefort – a blue-veined ewe's-milk cheese which comes from south-western France.

INGREDIENTS

Serves 4

225g/8oz pasta shapes

mixed salad leaves, such as rocket, curly endive, lamb's lettuce, baby spinach, radicchio, etc

30ml/2 tbsp walnut oil

60ml/4 tbsp sunflower oil

30ml/2 tbsp red wine vinegar or sherry vinegar

225g/8oz Roquefort cheese, roughly crumbled

115g/4oz/1 cup walnut halves

salt and ground black pepper

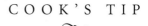

1 Cook the pasta in plenty of boiling salted water according to the instructions on the packet. Drain well and cool. Wash and dry the salad leaves and place them in a large bowl.

2 Whisk together the walnut oil, sunflower oil, vinegar and salt and pepper to taste.

3 Pile the pasta in the centre of the leaves, scatter over the crumbled Roquefort and pour over the dressing.

4 Scatter over the walnuts. Toss just before serving.

COOK'S TIP

Try toasting the walnuts under the grill for a couple of minutes to release the flavour.

Chicken and Pasta Salad

This is a delicious way to use up leftover cooked chicken, and makes a filling meal.

Serves 4

225g/8oz tri-coloured pasta twists

30ml/2 tbsp ready-made pesto sauce

15ml/1 tbsp olive oil

1 beefsteak tomato

12 stoned black olives

225g/8oz cooked French beans, cut into
    4cm/1½in lengths

350g/12oz cooked chicken, cubed

salt and ground black pepper

fresh basil, to garnish

1 Cook the pasta in plenty of boiling salted water according to the instructions on the packet.

2 Drain the pasta and rinse in plenty of cold running water. Put into a bowl and stir in the pesto sauce and olive oil.

3 Skin the tomato by placing it in boiling water for about 45 seconds and then into cold water, to loosen the skin.

4 Cut the tomato into small cubes and add to the pasta with the olives, seasoning and French beans. Add the cubed chicken. Toss gently together and transfer to a serving platter. Garnish with fresh basil.

Avocado, Tomato and Mozzarella Salad

This salad is made from ingredients representing the colours of the Italian flag – a sunny cheerful dish!

Serves 4

175g/6oz farfalle

6 ripe red tomatoes

225g/8oz mozzarella cheese

1 large ripe avocado

30ml/2 tbsp chopped fresh basil

30ml/2 tbsp pine nuts, toasted

fresh basil sprig, to garnish

For the dressing

90ml/6 tbsp olive oil

30ml/2 tbsp wine vinegar

5ml/1 tsp balsamic vinegar (optional)

5ml/1 tsp wholegrain mustard

pinch of sugar

salt and ground black pepper

1 Cook the pasta in plenty of boiling salted water according to the instructions on the packet. Drain well and cool.

4 Place all the dressing ingredients together in a small bowl and whisk until well blended.

2 Using a sharp knife slice the tomatoes and mozzarella cheese into thin rounds.

5 Arrange the sliced tomato, mozzarella and avocado overlapping around the edge of a flat serving plate.

3 Halve the avocado, remove the stone and peel off the skin. Slice the flesh lengthways.

6 Toss the pasta with half the dressing and the chopped basil. Pile into the centre of the plate. Pour over the remaining dressing, scatter over the pine nuts and garnish with a sprig of fresh basil. Serve immediately.

Pasta, Melon and Prawn Salad

Orange cantaloupe or Charentais melon look spectacular in this salad. Or try a mixture of ogen, cantaloupe and water melon.

Serves 4–6

175g/6oz pasta shapes

225g/8oz/2 cups frozen prawns, thawed and drained

1 large or 2 small melons

60ml/4 tbsp olive oil

15ml/1 tbsp tarragon vinegar

30ml/2 tbsp snipped fresh chives or chopped parsley

herb sprigs, to garnish

shredded Chinese leaves, to serve

1 Cook the pasta in boiling salted water according to the instructions on the packet. Drain well and allow to cool.

2 Peel the prawns and discard the shells.

3 Halve the melon and remove the seeds with a teaspoon. Carefully scoop the flesh into balls with a melon baller and mix with the prawns and pasta.

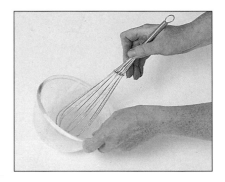

4 Whisk the oil, vinegar and chopped herbs together. Pour on to the prawn mixture and turn to coat. Cover and chill for at least 30 minutes.

5 Meanwhile shred the Chinese leaves and use to line a shallow bowl or the empty melon halves.

6 Pile the prawn mixture on to the Chinese leaves and garnish with sprigs of herbs.

Pasta Salad with Olives

This delicious salad combines all the flavours of the Mediterranean. It is an excellent way of serving pasta and is particularly suitable for a hot summer's day.

INGREDIENTS

Serves 6

450g/1lb short pasta, such as medium
   shells, farfalle or penne
60ml/4 tbsp extra virgin olive oil
10 sun-dried tomatoes, thinly sliced
30ml/2 tbsp capers, in brine or salted
115g/4oz/1 cup stoned black olives
2 garlic cloves, finely chopped
45ml/3 tbsp balsamic vinegar
45ml/3 tbsp chopped fresh parsley
salt and ground black pepper

1 Cook the pasta in plenty of boiling salted water until *al dente*. Drain and rinse under cold water to stop the cooking. Drain well and turn into a large bowl. Toss with the olive oil and set aside until required.

2 Soak the tomatoes in a bowl of hot water for 10 minutes. Do not discard the water. Rinse the capers well. If they have been preserved in salt, soak them in a little hot water for 10 minutes. Rinse again.

3 Combine the olives, tomatoes, capers, garlic and vinegar in a small bowl. Season with salt and ground black pepper.

4 Stir the olive mixture into the cooked pasta and toss well. Add 30–45ml/2–3 tbsp of the tomato soaking water if the salad seems too dry. Toss with the parsley and allow to stand for 15 minutes before serving.

Index